The Golden Principles

Here's to the pets we love, & the lessons they teach us. — Andy

What people are saying about The Golden Principles...

"In today's culture, there are many individuals who profess to understand leadership principles, yet there are very few who can articulate these leadership principles in a way that will stand the test of time. The Golden Principles deliver timeless truths that help leaders balance their hearts and their heads in order to influence others more effectively, both at work and at home."

Ron V. Sciarro
Master Franchisor, Aqua-Tots Swim Schools

"I have enjoyed watching Redford grow to love the Neillie family. This book wonderfully captures the power of relationships and the unspoken "words" we should live by, shown to us by these wonderful canines we know as 'Goldens'."

Dr. Erin Homburg
Redford's veterinarian

"Andy Neillie knows leadership. His character-based leadership principles have made him a popular coach for executives and leaders all over the world. Whether you lead a family, a scout troop, a PTA, a church, a small business or a Fortune 500, Andy's teachings on leadership in The Golden Principles will be well worth your investment. Buy this book. You'll be a better leader for it."

Dr. Will Davis Jr.
Senior Pastor, Austin Christian Fellowship

"The Golden Principles provide a refreshingly simple, humorous, yet profound way to look at and understand trusted leadership. Anyone striving for increased effectiveness in life through leadership must read this book."

Gene M. Ellerbee
Retired Senior Executive, The Procter & Gamble Company
Chairman, C12 Group-Austin

Dedication

To Alex, a prince among dogs.
You gave us a vision of what to expect.

To Kaibab, our Pygmalion.
Who says you can't teach an old dog new tricks?

To Trooper, the homeless.
You showed us dogs need hope as much as people do.

To Jodi, the beautiful.
Showgirl on the outside, mama's girl on the inside.

To Sammi, the relentless one.
You worked your way into our hearts.
(And any place else you wanted to go!)

To Ranger, country bumpkin with a heart of gold.
You always had room for one more.

To Maggie, the goofball.
Will you ever grow up?

To Smokey, who convinced us that cats were OK.
Even though I never really enjoyed sharing our bedroom
with another alpha male.

To Rascal, the lion-hearted.
It's not the size of the cat in the fight, but the size of
the fight in the cat.

To Nicholas, who never met someone
who wasn't a playmate.
Aren't kittens supposed to grow into cats?

To Lynn, who opened her heart to big dogs and aloof cats.
To Drew, who never met an animal she didn't like.

And most of all to Redford,
whose need has taught us so much.

The Golden Principles
Copyright ©2008 Andy Neillie
www.thegoldenprinciples.org
www.andyneillie.com

Layout & Design by Blooming Twig Books LLC
www.bloomingtwigbooks.com

Cover photograph copyright ©2008 Shawn Hatcher
For more information on Shawn's amazing photography,
Email him at *sshbiker@austin.rr.com*

Line drawings by Kristina Tosic.

Author's Special Edition

ISBN 978-1-933918-37-2

Table of Contents

Money will buy a fine dog,
but only love will make him wag his tail

Golden Principle
Number One

It doesn't matter how much you love someone,
it takes time for your love to be trusted.

It all started under the porch…

R edford was getting on my nerves. Let me explain.

We have a large porch on the back of our home, with several steps leading down to the yard. The steps are 12 feet wide and provide not just steps down to the yard, but a place to sit when we have poolside get-togethers in our backyard. My wife Lynn and I have always liked how wide the steps are – they open up the porch and make a graceful transition from our house to our yard.

This afternoon, Redford, our recently adopted Golden Retriever, wedged himself underneath these very same steps halfway between each end – six feet away from either of us being able to reach him. Not only was he six feet away from our reach, he was laying in a pool of muddy water.

I needed to leave for the airport immediately, and every minute I tried to get Redford to come out from under the steps moved me closer to missing my business flight. To compound the problem, it was raining *cats and dogs*.

Redford came to us by way of a Golden Retriever rescue group in Houston, Texas. These groups are located all across the country, and they specialize in placing abandoned, abused or homeless Golden Retrievers with new families. This particular rescue group was part of an emergency nationwide effort to save 66 *Goldens* (as we Golden Retriever owners affectionately name the breed) who had been abused and neglected at a puppy mill in Arkansas in the fall of 2004. A puppy mill is essentially a large-scale breeding factory, where dogs are mistreated and misused until they become "useless" to the breeder. When organizations rescue dogs from puppy mills, they often spend a great deal of time rehabilitating the dogs, and they search for caring and nurturing families to take care of them.

Our new rescued Golden had probably never been called by his original name. And, when one of the rescue group leaders saw, even in his mangy state, that he had a beautiful red coat, they named him "Redford."

We loved Redford from the minute we saw him. But Redford didn't yet know how to appreciate it. He didn't realize that we would take him home and provide for him. He couldn't possibly understand that he would never again lack a roof over his head, and always have good food and a safe environment.

E ven when we did take care of Redford consistently and surely he still didn't quite get it. He continued to run and hide for weeks and even months to his various *caves* (our name for his hiding places) and to the place under the steps where we had so much trouble getting him out that day before my trip.

The good news is that he started to hide less frequently as time went by. It has now been more than three years since we rescued Redford, and indeed, it is the *time* that we've spent with him that has helped him to slowly understand…

Our love hasn't changed, but now, when he comes running at our call, tail wagging and goofy Golden Retriever-grin on his face *(yes, dogs do smile!)*, we can see that his trust of our love has grown.

Prior to being rescued, Redford most likely spent his days living in a 2-foot by 3-foot crate, only being let out to eat, go to the bathroom and to be used as a breeding sire. The first time I approached him, he cowered and put his tail between his legs. I suspect he had been abused during his puppy mill days, and he will always carry that fear with him. While less scared around women and children, Redford still doesn't easily display the joy and affection born into all Golden Retrievers. We've adopted seven Goldens in the past twenty years, and we had faith that, with love and consistency, he would come out of his shell.

One week Redford was barely surviving in a squalid puppy mill, and the next week he had won what you might call the *doggie lottery.* Our house is ideal for a young Golden:

- *We have a large yard with lots of room to run and romp.*

- *I'm convinced at times our in-ground pool is more for the Goldens than our family members – they can swim and play all day long,*

- *We take our dogs on regular walks and runs,*

- *They get to go on frequent trips to the local ice cream parlor that gives out free "puppy cups,"*

- *They lounge on a sleeping pad by the master bedroom,*

- *They feast on good food,*

- *They are showered by lots of affection,*

- *And they have a loving family who will spend whatever we need to on top-quality veterinarian care.*

…What a life!

Here's the challenge – Redford didn't get it. He didn't know how lucky he was. He had no idea how good we would be to him. And so that rainy Sunday afternoon, he wedged himself underneath the porch, muddy and wet, trying to hide from us because he didn't trust us.

W ell, eventually we got Redford out from under the steps. Some muddy jeans and wet clothes, a number of very dirty towels, mud on hands and knees, and the job was done. We got him cleaned up, dried off and back into the house. I even got to the airport in time for my flight.

Three years have gone by since the incident under the steps. But Redford still doesn't completely trust us. Just last night I stepped into the hallway where Redford was laying. My shoe made a slight noise as it hit the tiled hallway floor, and Redford jumped and took off running for the desk in our kitchen – one of the caves he takes refuge in.

Until Redford fully trusts us, he won't be able to fully experience his new freedoms and joy. As I reflected on Redford's personality and response to us, it slowly dawned on me that his response to us is oftentimes also our response to people around us. While Redford needs to learn lots of new life lessons from us, I've also come to realize that there are important life lessons we all need to learn from him.

Indeed, Golden Principle #1 developed out of my realization that Redford was hiding under the porch because of a critically important life truth:

Golden Principle #1

It doesn't matter how much you love someone, it takes time for your love to be trusted.

T wo thousand years before we adopted Redford, Greek was the *lingua franca* of the day. Used by business leaders and scholars alike, it became the first universal language across the known world.

Ancient Greek was a rich and nuanced language. Our word *time*, so vital to Golden Principle #1, was represented by several nuanced words in Greek.

Chronos was the common word for time in ancient Greek. We get *chronology* and *chronometer* from this word. *Chronos* represented calendar time. The day-in, day-out passage of regular time.

A second Greek word is translated into English as *time*, but with a much richer meaning. *Kairos* meant "special time" or "opportunity time." Used more sparingly in ancient Greek writings, it was the word that captured the significance of a specific moment in time.

CHRONOS: *The passage of time.*

KAIROS: *Specific or appointed time.*

Recently my teenage daughter Drew asked me to go on a neighborhood bike ride. Unfortunately, I was on deadline for a work project, and was hard at work in my home office when she poked her head in and made the request. The deadline was looming; the amount of *Chronos* (the passage of time) left for completion was slipping through my fingers literally moment-by-moment.

I also recognized that time with Drew was fleeting; she would be in college is three short years. So I pushed the work aside, pushed myself away from the desk, pumped up the tires, and joined her in an hour-long bike ride.

Thirty minutes into our leisurely ride, Drew started talking. Not just chatting, but really talking. About life as a teenager. About peer pressure. About school, studies, friends and fears.

Everyone knows the importance of *quality time*. What I recognized that afternoon was that you only get *quality time* when you spend *quantity* time. In this case, *Kairos* (quality time) only happened as a result of *Chronos* (the passage of time). *Chronos* and *Kairos* build the foundation of our time, and our time goes to build trust in our relationships.

CHRONOS	➡	**KAIROS**
Quantity time		*Quality time*

What was true for Drew and Redford is also always true for any intimate relationships: the power of our love is directly tied to the amount of time we spend with those we love.

Golden Principle #1 also applies to leaders as they seek to lead their organizations. While the bonds of love may be too powerful to consider in a work environment, this principle can also be stated in a more general way:

It doesn't matter how much you care for someone, it takes time for your care to be trusted.

Effective leaders know the value of the time they spend with those they lead and influence. There is a direct correlation between the time they spend and the impact they have on their organizations.

A study by the *Corporate Executive Board* in 2006 found that sales leaders who purposefully dedicated more than five hours per month to one-on-one coaching with each of their sales professionals saw a fifteen percent increase in sales closing. Sales professionals went from *missing* their sales targets by 8% to *exceeding* their goals by 7%.

The challenge for most leaders is not that they *choose* to not spend time with the people reporting to them. The challenge is the busy work schedule leaders find themselves immersed in.

In the last twenty years, the pace of a leader's life, and the management responsibilities placed upon most organizational leaders, has increased so significantly that making time for the people around them has become a huge challenge. Furthermore, in addition to the management responsibilities most leaders must fulfill, many leaders find themselves being player-coaches: not only do they have a team they lead, they have their own goals and responsibilities that they are held accountable for.

How can a leader address the challenge of finding time for the people he/she intends to positively influence? It takes commitment, purposefulness and hard work.

Many effective leaders I've interviewed block regular time off on their busy calendars for each one of their protégés. Team members will be motivated by the knowledge that they have a set meeting scheduled to give them an opportunity to meet with their manager. Gene Kent, a sales leader for the technology giant Cisco Systems, calls these his *one-on-one* times with his team. Once he instituted these regularly scheduled times, he saw the productivity of his team skyrocket. Their trust factor increases with the employment of *Chronos* and *Kairos*.

Others leaders are committing themselves to use technology effectively to be available to their team members. Instant messaging, text messaging, email, voicemail and web-enabled communication technologies allow leaders to be readily available to team members, even if their team members are in remote locations. Recently I spoke with a team leader who manages people across fourteen time zones on three continents. He relies extensively on technology to stay in touch with each of his team members.

For leaders who lead in close proximity to their protégés, a consistent open door policy and a habit of "managing by walking around" go a long way toward raising their visibility and effectiveness.

Effective leaders also learn the power of delegation. They know they can sometimes delegate non-critical activities to other *people*. Just as importantly, they know they can oftentimes delegate non-critical activities to other *times*. This habit of delegation frees them up to have more time to be available for the people around them, building trust in the workplace.

I n my study of effective leaders, I've noticed a practice that many leaders follow almost unconsciously. I call this practice their *Trust Account* - not a trust account like a wealthy individual might establish for his or her family, but a relational trust account between a *leader* and a *follower*.

Every leader has many relational trust accounts. Each account reflects the relationship the leader has with each person he or she influences. Leaders make deposits into these accounts and withdrawals from these accounts. Wise leaders recognize the need to have a positive balance in each one of their followers' trust accounts against which they can later make withdrawals.

There are two powerful axioms tied to each one of these trust accounts:

Axiom #1

Deposits, by their very nature, are typically *small*. It is hard to make a large deposit. Trust is only earned over time. It truly is the little things that count.

Axiom #2

Withdrawals, by their very nature, are typically *large*. Any time a leader asks a follower to do something, it is a withdrawal. Any time a hard decision is implemented, it is a withdrawal. Changes in strategic goals or methods to implement them are withdrawals. A difficult personnel issue is a withdrawal.

In today's pressure-cooker business environment, leaders are required to make withdrawals regularly. As a result of these axioms, it is the wise leader that recognizes the importance of making regular, consistent deposits into each of his or her protégés Trust Accounts.

leader who is committed to practicing Golden Principle #1 is continually asking himself or herself six critical leadership questions:

1. *What am I doing that doesn't need to be done by me, or doesn't need to be done by me right now? How can I free up time from these things for my subordinates?*

2. *How can I arrange my schedule to be more available to my team members?*

3. *Who do I need to specifically reach out to this week? In what way?*

4. *How can I incorporate relationship-building into my existing schedule – are there activities this week I can make joint activities with members of my team?*

5. *What can I do to reinforce my intention to be available to team members who need my time? How can I better communicate that intention?*

6. *What* Trust Account *deposits do I need to make this week?*

Effective leaders ask themselves these types of questions regularly. They intuitively know the challenge of *Chronos* and *Kairos*, and practice Golden Principle #1 as a way to increase their leadership influence.

We've had Redford more than three years now. How's he doing? Better.

Redford still loses it at times. He still runs and hides in one of his "caves." Truth is, he may never be completely without fear. But our *time* with Redford is allowing him to *trust* our love.

I came home late at night from the airport after a recent business trip, waking the whole house at my arrival. In the past, that late-night interruption would have sent Redford running for cover. Not this time. He was right there greeting me with all the other members of my family.

Redford was happy to see me.

LEADERSHIP APPLICATION

Golden Principle Number One

It doesn't matter how much you love someone,
it takes time for your love to be trusted.

1. Who do you know who does a good job of applying this principle?

2. What two or three specific things do they do to live out this principle?

3. What challenges do you face in living out this principle?

4. What two or three specific things can you begin doing in order to better live out this principle?

Golden Principle Number Two

If you really want to reach someone,
you have to get down to their level.

A late night play-bow…

I t had been another hectic afternoon followed by a long, late-night flight. I rushed to the airport after a training engagement went late, hurried through security (can anybody "hurry" through security anymore?), went straight to the boarding gate and managed to get on the plane right before they closed the doors.

Fighting for overhead space for my roll-aboard, I squeezed into my middle seat "in the back of the bus," only to discover that both men on either side of me had requested seat-belt extenders because of their large girths. I was pinched on both sides.

Fortunately, several *squeezed* hours later I made it home. As I pulled into the garage I let out a sigh of relief. Walking in the door, I dropped my suitcase and briefcase, raised my arms and announced in a loud voice that boomed throughout the whole house for the entire family to hear, "I'm ho-ome!"

I figured since the *primary bread-winner* was back *at last* after another victorious endeavor putting bread on the table and holding the creditors at bay, everyone should come running in rapt adulation for the alpha male who had now triumphantly returned to his domain.

I was wrong on two counts:

1. Nobody but me seemed to be overly impressed with my arrival.

2. Everybody just kept sleeping except Redford. As soon as I walked in the door and boomed out, "I'm ho-ome," Redford went running for cover.

Normally our dogs sleep in the hallway right by our bedroom door, which also happens to be the hallway where we enter from the garage. Well, as soon as I dropped my bags and raised my voice, Redford, who had been sleeping peacefully by the bedroom until I arrived, took off for one of his caves.

Redford has two caves in our house – one is under the desk that Lynn uses in our home office. He likes this cave because he can be close to her and still look out on the rest of the house from behind the glass French doors that she closes when she is on the phone or doing client work.

Redford's other cave is under the built-in desk in our kitchen. He likes this cave because it is small and enclosed, and he can hide in there when we are working in the kitchen, close enough to see and hear us as we prepare meals, but squeezed far enough back that he is protected from all the hustle-and-bustle.

His kitchen cave is the hiding spot Redford went running towards as I burst through the door that evening. As soon as I saw him go running, I remembered what I had done and realized my mistake.

Redford doesn't do well with loud noises and alpha males.

H ave you ever watched dogs in large groups? I hadn't either, until we got Redford. Near our home is a dog park where you are allowed to take your dogs off-leash and let them run and play. It is along a creek, and many of the dogs romp through the water as they play with one another.

Dogs have complex social norms to which most of us are completely oblivious. When they first greet one another, there is the sniffing – *checking each other out*. Eye contact is very important for a dog. Overall posture – shoulders, tail – it all communicates what we humans say in words.

One of the particular stances that communicates a certain message is a dog's *play-bow*. You've seen dogs do play-bows whenever you've seen a dog get up from laying down, stretch their legs out in front of them, looking up, tail wagging, to say a happy "hi." That posture - when a dog stretches his front legs out in front of him, lowering his head and shoulders, back legs up and tail wagging - is a play-bow. Play-bows say "I like you, I'm happy to see you, can we play together?"

It wasn't too long after we got Redford that we sought out professional help to try and understand his behavior and how we could reach his fearful heart. Here in Austin, Texas, there is a legend in the dog world, Melissa. She and her husband own several boarding kennels and do dog training. They've been doing it for years, and have quite a following of people who love their pets and bring

Melissa their challenging canine behavioral issues. I call Melissa the local *dog whisperer*. At our request, Melissa came and spent time with our family and Redford. She got to know him, she gave us some recommendations on how to train him, and she taught us the importance of the play-bow.

Melissa taught us that for Redford to get comfortable with us, he needed to know that we were "safe." He was looking, in the language he understands, for cues from us that we were on his side. That means he was looking for our body language to tell him that we were not a threat.

Unfortunately, walking straight in from the garage, striding into the hallway, and booming out "I'm ho-ome" was exactly the wrong approach to communicate to him that I was on his side. So, despite my best intentions to connect with Redford, I was unknowingly appearing to be a threat every time I got home.

Here's what I do now. I walk into the house, get down on my hands and knees, and do a human version of a play-bow. Then Redford, our other dogs and I wrestle on the floor for a few minutes. Tails are wagging, tongues are licking, smiles are being shared, and I'm getting eye contact – warm eye contact, from my dogs. Redford knows I'm safe.

Without thinking about it, I'm demonstrating Golden Principle number two:

> *If you really want to reach someone,*
> *you have to get down to their level.*

This principle has far-ranging implications. From the dad who kneels down to talk to his three year-old, to the model of Jesus, who was *a friend to sinners*, to the high-level retail manager who comes in and pulls floor shifts during the busy Christmas season, leaders earn the right to lead when their followers sense they are *down in the trenches* with them.

J on Sullivan is a professional massage therapist. He practices *myofascial release*. While he has talked to me about the essence of myofascial release, I have no real idea what he does exactly when he touches a patient. But I know it works. I'm not sure if it is the myofascial release that really works, or if it is simply Jon's ability to connect with your body's aches and pains somehow.

I'm not a mystical person by nature, and I tend to shy away from the supernatural, so I can't really explain Jon's touch. I have a very high opinion of God, and know that the bible talks about God giving spiritual gifts to his followers - I even know that the bible talks about healing as one of those gifts. But the whole concept just seems strange and otherworldly to me. But I have to admit there is something about Jon's touch. When he massages you, you get better. I've experienced it, and I've seen it in a number of people. I just don't know what to make of it.

Here's what I do know: Jon will tell you he is doing what he was born to do. It is not just his job, it is his purpose in life — his "calling." And it requires him to touch you. His influence is only felt when he is in physical contact with you. I think that is true with all effective leadership – it requires that same kind of personal touch.

A nyone who is a good parent of young children intuitively understands the principle of touch and connection. Because parents want to truly connect with their children, we kneel down to their level. We get on our hands and knees so that we are eye-to-eye with them.

We could bend over at the waist and towered over our children, but instead we hunker down so that they find it easier to reach out for us. They smile at us. They share their toys. They learn to trust us.

Conversely, people who try exploit their position over the people around them will often find their influence minimized. I had a friend in college who was a good athlete. At 6'4", he towered over just about everyone. He always shook hands in such a way that his hand was on top – he leaned in and over you while he was shaking your hand. It felt like a subtle way of saying, "I'm bigger than you. I'm probably better than you." This opening handshake often drove people away from him. His ability to influence was compromised because he wasn't willing to meet people where they were.

When you greet people do you want to make a *powerful* impression? The best leaders don't care about making a powerful impression but instead about *putting others at ease*.

Pope John Paul II was a leader who understood the need to connect with his people. While he was a strict moralist who strongly reaffirmed the conservative positions of the Catholic church, he was well-loved because of his human touch. During his time as Pope, he traveled more than 700,000 miles on more than 100 foreign trips so that he could be among his people. It was his touch that made him an effective leader.

I f you lead any type of organization today, you recognize that the environment has changed in the last decade. There are three realities I see in the current work environment, and when you put these realities together, it will lead you to the conclusion that effective leadership requires each of us to practice Golden Principle number two.

Leadership Reality #1:

All organizations in today's marketplace are volunteer organizations. Whether you are a leader inside a technology company, a non-profit, a government agency, a service firm, a sales team or old-line manufacturing company, your people work for you of their own free will. If things get too bad, they will leave.

Leadership Reality #2:

You can't lead a volunteer organization with traditional command-and-control dynamics. Gone are the days of order-giving bosses and order-taking subordinates. Your team will rebel against an ivory-tower leadership model. They expect you to be with them in their efforts.

Leadership Reality #3:

The only sustainable leadership model for long-term success is one based on informal power - the power of influence. This is why effective leaders get down to the level of their team members. That is where real influence is felt – in the trenches, as you get close to your team members – as you touch them in their world.

Ron Sciarro is the president of three companies. He is a very busy man. Millions of dollars pass under his authority annually. Budgets, staffing, contracts and facilities are always on his plate. Yet you can also find him regularly behind the sales counter, working directly with his people, reaching out directly to his customers. He understands these three leadership realities, and is committed to connecting regularly with those he intends to influence.

"My people need to be in dialogue with me, and I need to be in dialogue with them," Ron said when I spoke with him about this recently.

"The thing I'm learning is how time with my employees is so vital to their success. The time they have with me acts as a catalyst to the staff that is actually doing the work - my small investment is magnified by the work they do. I don't actually do the work, but I catalyze their work by talking about the end result and the vision of what they are trying to accomplish, reassuring them and reigniting them that what they do is important.

"At the office, I spend my mornings preparing and doing the things that only I can do, so in the afternoon I'm available for 1-on-1s and meetings with staff for whatever they need. During those meetings, I ask a lot of open-ended questions, giving them time to bring up the things that are on their minds.

"These 1-on-1 meetings, where I get down to their level, are great opportunities to dialogue about the conflicts my employees are running in to. Recently one of my people had the opportunity to enter us into a contract that would have been very lucrative for us, but risked going into a grey area of contract compliance. Through our discussions, she was able to see that this wasn't some-thing we wanted to do because it would risk violating our core val-ues. Only by "being in the trenches" with her was I able to help her understand that her good intentions needed to be tempered by the bigger picture of the company."

This principle of *being in the trenches* is also epitomized by basketball phenom Steve Nash.

S teve Nash is the team captain and play-maker guard for the NBA Phoenix Suns, and a two-time NBA MVP. He leads a team of high-performers, and has been recognized as one of the best guards playing professional basketball currently and perhaps of all time. While Steve is a strong scorer, he is primarily known for his passing, assists and overall floor leadership abilities.

Because I travel so much, I have enough frequent flyer status that I get upgraded to first class regularly, where I get to ride with some interesting people. Recently I sat next to Steve Nash for an hour and got to ask him about his take on the importance of connecting as a leadership. Here are some of the thoughts I took away:

> 1. *In leading a new team, don't come in with a big ego. Come on with maturity. Be fun – particularly if you can have fun at your own expense. Leaders should laugh at themselves, and laugh along with their players. They have to feel you care.*

> 2. *In order for players to trust their leader, the leader has to first trust him/herself. There are times when a team leader (like Steve) will take the shot because he trusts himself to make it. There are other times when he passes the basketball to someone else – and they know he is giving it to them because he trusts them with the ball.*

> 3. *Most importantly, trust is earned through passion and motives. When your motives are pure, the rest of your team sees that and knows you are real. You don't have to be a* rah-rah *leader. But you do have to be selfless. You don't have to have an aura of leadership. There were a lot of times during Steve's*

season when he was quiet. But you have to be yourself. Be real – that's the only way you can be more acute about your goal and get the whole team focused on it.

4. *If a player blows it, that isn't the time for you as a leader to drop your shoulders and scowl at them. You may need to encourage them a bit. Or maybe you just need to act as if it was no big deal. You have to practice forgiveness and be an encourager. Other people on the team pick those things up.*

5. *Body language is very important – people read a great deal from your body language. How a leader responds can help them know how to respond, based on what they see you doing.*

6. *You may not always agree with your management. As a team leader, it is important to both support management and let your team know that you don't cower at times. Steve talked about walking around the locker room at times, trying to lighten things up on purpose after the coaches got down on them, in order to help team members.*

7. *Your team needs to see you going in the right direction.*

8. *If you as a leader need to call someone out, try very hard to do so without violating their*

*trust. Steve tries to do it in private, which can
be tough to do on the basketball court. He
will tell them what they need to do, what they
are doing and how it needs to change, and
tries to find a way to encourage them about
something they are doing well.*

9.   *Trust is earned when they see you doing it.
Before Steve's first year with the Suns, he
spent the entire month of September in Phoenix, before training camp, working his tail
off. The rest of the team saw that. He didn't
do it so that they would see him – he just
knew that was what he needed to do. When
the team got to training camp, his teammates
all knew how hard he had been working. A
leader has to work incredibly hard – it is that
hard work that earns their players' trust. And
you have to learn to read your team.*

I realized several months ago that I liked getting down on
the floor with my dogs. In fact, not only do I enjoy it, it
is a great way to relieve stress. Every time I get home,
we all get to play for a few minutes together. Walk in the
door. Kiss my wife. Hug my daughter. Then into the kitchen,
where there's enough room for three dogs and one alpha male to
get down on the floor, stretch, smile and make connection. All of
the sudden, the pressures of the world seem smaller and more
manageable.

LEADERSHIP APPLICATION

Golden Principle Number Two

If you really want to reach someone,
you have to get down to their level.

1. *Who do you know who does a good job of applying this principle?*

2. *What two or three specific things do they do to live out this principle?*

3. *What challenges do you face in living out this principle?*

4. *What two or three specific things can you begin doing in order to better live out this principle?*

Golden Principle Number Three

Positive reinforcement always works better than negative reinforcement.

Redford was a runner. That's a bad thing…

"Redford, NOOOOO!" I yelled it again as he was bolting out the garage door. Redford had this bad habit of running out of the garage whenever we opened the door remotely from inside the car as we were pulling up.

Our home is set up so that there is a doggie-door from the house into the garage, and another one from the garage to the back yard. Though a little complicated, the system works well as long as the garage doors are closed.

I yelled at Redford for months, every time I came home, opened the garage door. And Redford kept running for months. My negative approach wasn't working. It was time to try another approach. But how do you keep a dog from running when you aren't right there with him? You're in the car, pulling into the driveway.

We could close the doggie-door between the house and the garage, but that defeats the whole purpose of the doggie-door. Besides, that didn't really address his behavior. We could avoid using the garage door opener, and instead park on the curb, enter through the front door, secure Redford and then go back out to pull the car in. But that would be such a hassle. And again, that solution would do nothing to address the behavior - it simply avoids the problem.

What was the solution, after much head-scratching and many trials? Don't address the wrong behavior at all.

Instead of reprimanding Redford when he did what we didn't like, we needed to find the right behavior and reinforce it. The correct behavior for Redford would be to stay in the house, or at the least, come to us in the car when we came home – not run into the street.

Now, when I come home, I make sure I roll my car window down, and as soon as I start pulling the car in, I start calling Redford's name. I act so excited to see him that he prefers coming to me at the car rather than running into the street. I make it a *Redford, Dad-is-home-love-fest*! He can't wait for me to get out of the car. In fact, he stands right by the car door until I open it, so that he can put his paws on the doorsill and his head in my lap. He loves it! And most importantly, he's not running.

Without purposefully invoking it, this stay-in-the-car-and-urge-Redford-to-come-tome behavior was a natural expression of Golden Principle #3:

Positive reinforcement always works better than negative reinforcement.

It took me a while to figure it out, but this positive reinforcement is stock-and-trade for most good animal trainers. It doesn't always work to focus on eliminating wrong behaviors. Many times, the best thing to do is to reward right behaviors. Everybody loves a love-fest!

A number of years ago, I was at the receiving end of this type of positive reinforcement. At that time, I was the Director of Student Services for Phoenix Seminary, a new, innovative graduate theology school in the Valley of the Sun. Bill Yarger was the Vice President of the seminary at that time, and the finest manager I ever worked for. He set clear expectations for me and then gave me the freedom to do my job. We were partners, if you will, in the work. While he was clearly my superior, he made our work a collaborative effort.

Spring was always the most important recruiting season for the seminary, and I headed up an initiative that had all of us on the executive team working very hard to meet with as many interested prospects as possible. As part of the process, I developed and updated an Excel spreadsheet that helped us monitor where we were at any time in the process. The spreadsheet was simple, but it became crucial because it helped us with our forecasting. The numbers on the spreadsheet needed to be tallied and consulted almost daily as they determined plans for the next year: which classes to offer when, how many sections of which classes, etc.

One particularly hectic day I was out of the office, busy with the day-to-day demands of prospect meetings, and I didn't get the numbers in at our agreed-to time. When Bill called me to ask for them, I gave him a series of flimsy excuses that didn't approach the reality that I just hadn't made it a priority as I should have.

The next day, I apologized to Bill for my behavior. I was embarrassed for having not only missed the deadline but also for not being upfront and honest with him.

Bill could have turned my failure and apology into *an ethical lapse* for a seminary employee, but instead he was affirming. He thanked me for my honesty, talked with me about what we needed to do to make sure we had those critically important numbers when we needed them, and then he had us move on. No guilt; no re-criminations – just a reinforcement of the good work he knew I could do. And he gave me a great quote that I'll never forget:

"If you have to eat crow (and we all do),
at least eat is while it is still warm."

Several years ago, I was involved in a leadership training initiative that drove home this principle of positive rein-forcement over negative reinforcement. The work was for a major bank in the western US. In addition to the work we were doing for this company, they hired a consulting firm to research best practices among their managers and team leaders. One of the studies the consulting firm presented found that the bank managers who scored highest in an employee survey demonstrated a 5-to-1 ratio between positive affirmations and criticisms.

When I first reviewed their report, I must confess I thought it was "over the top" and couldn't quite believe their findings. That even exceeds the commonly cited 80-20 rule so prevalent in mod-ern business theory. As I drilled further down into their research, however, what became apparent to me was that the best managers didn't purposefully approach their respective team members with 5 "atta-boys" before they offered any constructive criticism. Rather, the best managers in this firm made positive affirmations a way of performing their leadership.

These leaders were continually making *deposits* into each of their employees' trust accounts. Those deposits, when analyzed in the study, were five times more prevalent than corrective disci-pline. They understood the power of positive reinforcement.

Doug Conant is the CEO of Campbell Soup Co. In the years he's led Campbell's, he has turned the stodgy old brand into a market leader in innovation and a growth machine.

His leadership approach is a wonderful combination of humility and drive. On one hand, he's not afraid to make tough decisions. On the other hand, he has sent out more than 16,000 handwritten thank-you notes during his tenure at Campbell's. Talk about positive reinforcement!

He focuses his energies on four people-oriented keys:

1. Use a personal touch.

2. Set clear, regular expectations.

3. Be open to other opinions.

4. Create opportunities for movement and change.

A great leader focuses on the good in others and seeks ways to praise what has been done. If they rule with an *iron fist*, then the iron fist most definitely has a *velvet glove* over it. They almost never belittle. But they are also straightforward about what is expected. If there are problems, they deal with them. If expectations are not being met, they address them. But they never belittle; a great leader finds the positive and reinforces it.

I recently worked with a leader that typified this positive approach. Andrew Choi is a business consultant and coach in Asia, and works with other business leaders to develop their leadership potential. We were together at a leadership training engagement in Beijing. In my brief work with Andrew, he embodied all the things I find so appealing about the effective Asian leader. He was clearly in charge of the program he and I worked on together, yet he never asserted his position. He was deferential without being overly solicitous. Furthermore, he was well-prepared, confident and encouraging, other-oriented and positive.

Andrew has a very gracious demeanor, captured by that most Asian of traditions - he always bows slightly to me when we greet.

The bow is a subtle, but effective positive reinforcement of our relationship, and displays both respect and honor. His bowing is not over the top. Neither is it fake. It simply is a genuine reflection of his graciousness - I can tell he means me well, and respects me. When it is done genuinely, like Andrew does it, it is a warm and honoring act. Maybe we should start bowing to our team members in this country as well. (I have now even learned to play-bow with Redford at home, as was noted in an earlier chapter.)

T hese types of positive reinforcement also work in our neighborhoods. At least when you have neighbors like Baba and Shenal.

We mean well. We really do. We want to be good neighbors. We mow our lawn, we bring our trash cans in on time. We don't let our teenage daughter have any wild parties in our cul-de-sac. (Okay, that's not fair; she's not really the partying type).

But we are less than ideal neighbors.

Redford barks when we are gone - a lot. Furthermore, his barking isn't the friendly "I have a ball - don't you want to come over and play?" bark of the typical Golden. Because of the abuse in his past, he carries the fear of men, and his bark is a warning: "Don't come near; I don't trust you; I have to protect myself."

To make matters worse, we have a wrought iron fence that he can see through, so he barks even more whenever he sees someone approaching our house or yard. And our next-door neighbors, who have two young children, have taken to playing in their front yard instead of their back yard because of his threatening barks.

To add to our neighborly demeanor, our pool equipment is on the far side of our house, right next to these same neighbors' house; more importantly, right next to their master bedroom. Last winter it got unusually cold in Austin - below freezing several nights. So the freeze protection built into our automatic pool pump turned itself on and ran all night.

I was gone on a business trip, and wasn't aware that not only was the pump on all night every night, but one of the pump bearings was going bad, turning the relatively quiet drone of the pump into a relatively loud, high-pitched squeal. Right next to our neighbors' bedroom window. All night long.

Not only did they not say anything about it to us; when I apologized, our neighbor expressed concern for us, knowing something was wrong with some of the equipment at our house, and hoping that there was no damage. They always act that way: concerned for Redford, even though he is a "problem child." Wanting to bring soup over when somebody in our family is sick, bringing packages in for us when they are left on the front doorstep too long, and so on. Needless to say, I got the pool equipment fixed as soon as possible.

Indeed, these neighbors are two of the most gracious people we know. Their graciousness as neighbors earns them respect. I listen when they speak. I will do my best to be a good neighbor to them because their graciousness has earned them the right to influence my home-ownership decisions. Their positive reinforcement makes me want to be an exemplary neighbor.

The Greek scribe Aesop captured the power of positive reinforcement several thousand years ago in his fable of the Wind and the Sun. As his story goes, the Wind and the Sun were disputing which was stronger. Suddenly they saw a traveler coming down the road, and the Sun said: "I see a way to decide our dispute. Whichever of us can cause that traveler to take off his cloak shall be regarded as the stronger. You begin." So the Sun retired behind a cloud, and the Wind began to blow as hard as it could upon the traveler. But the harder he blew the more closely the traveler wrapped his cloak round him, until at last the Wind had to give up in despair. Then the Sun came out and shone in all his glory upon the traveler, who soon found it too warm to need to walk with his cloak on. The moral of this fable: kindness always has a more positive effect than severity.

Maggie is our newest dog, a big, likeable Labrador-Shepherd mix. Unlike most of our other pets, she was adopted, but we didn't rescue her out of a horrible situation. Instead, we took her from a very good situation. She came happy, healthy, and emotionally well-adjusted, unlike Redford, who came to us with a lot of doggie baggage.

Maggie came from a disability-training center, where she was being trained to work as a service dog. Unfortunately, she "flunked" her final exam because she wasn't quite up to the standards of a service dog (something about doggie ADD - Maggie has a very short attention span). As a result, the training agency wouldn't place her as a service dog. She is a great pet, though, and pretty well-trained. At least when she is on leash and paying attention to you. Unfortunately, her ADD-ness, combined with her natural puppy energy, sometimes get the best of her. Like last month at the creek.

During the hot summer months, the creek is a popular hang-out for lots of people, and one day recently, one of the other people at the creek was throwing a tennis ball for his dog to retrieve. Well, party-animal Maggie wanted to get in on the action, and took off to join the tennis-ball event. Despite our constant calling of her name, she wouldn't come back to us.

So here was a dilemma: how could I find positive reinforcement to get Maggie to *want* to come back to me? If I yell angrily, that will make her want to stay away even more, perhaps even making her afraid of me. But my calm and rational appeals don't seem to work either – she is having too much fun with the tennis-ball crowd to want to come back to me. It isn't even Maggie's fault: if I was a two year-old ball-crazy dog, I would want to be doing the tennis-ball-in-the-creek thing myself.

That's when it hit me: positive reinforcement often takes pre-planning. I should have anticipated ahead of time that we might run into someone playing ball with their dog – we've seen them before. I probably should have thought to bring our own ball and be prepared to make Maggie want to come back to us because of the fun she might miss with our ball.

I suspect that most good leaders, if you ask them about positive reinforcement, will share with you that it doesn't just happen. They have to very consciously make it happen, and prepare in advance, in order for it to work.

A nd that brings me back to Redford.
To get him to quit running, I had to be prepared. It took purposeful planning to reinforce the positive, but it worked. So well, in fact, that it is now a pleasure each time I come home to know that Redford will be excited by my arrival, eagerly coming towards my car door instead of racing into

the street. I don't restrict his freedom, and he doesn't want to break the rules. On the contrary, he wants to do it right!

With our Goldens, pre-emptive positive reinforcement is worth its weight in gold.

LEADERSHIP APPLICATION

Golden Principle Number Three
Positive reinforcement always works better
than negative reinforcement.

1. Who do you know who does a good job of applying this principle in their communication?

2. What two or three specific things do they do to demonstrate this principle?

3. What challenges do you face in practicing this principle?

4. What two or three specific things can you begin doing in order to reach who you really need to reach?

Golden Principle Number Four

Always know who your most important audience is.

It really all started with Alex.

We bought our first house in Ahwatukee, Arizona, a bedroom community just south of Phoenix, in 1984. No more apartment living! Close to the freeway, close to the mountain preserve, and most importantly, with a back yard. A fenced back yard - large enough for a dog.

Unfortunately, it wasn't very long into the dog discussion that Lynn and I reached an impasse in our marriage. "Dog" to me meant big, happy, goofy – the kind of dog you could roll on the floor with, take on long runs, put in the back of a pickup truck to take to Home Depot. A real man's dog.

Conversely, "dog" to Lynn meant small, gentle, polite - the kind of dog that never dug in the mud, that sat quietly on the couch while we watched TV, that waited to be asked before it crossed from the tiled family room into the carpeted bedroom. A lady's dog.

Despite my best persuasive power, I wasn't winning this argument. According to Lynn, we were not going to have the kind of dog "...that puts its paws on the kitchen counter, brings mud in the house, and sticks its nose in impolite places!"

My vision of a Golden or Lab was quickly losing momentum to a small, scruffy thing that you would never take with you to Home Depot or a pick-up football game with the guys.

Despite our lack of agreement on the "dog-ness" of a dog, we moved forward with the process. We had a family friend who was a vet, and we put the word out through him that we were looking for a good dog that needed a good home. Several weeks went by, and then we heard that a dog had been found in the desert north of Phoenix. A couple who loved dogs had taken him into their home until a permanent home could be found.

Here's the bad news: Alex (the name this couple gave him) was a Golden Retriever – which I knew was a big, happy, goofy breed; the exact kind Lynn was dead-set against. Here's the good news: their home was a full 45 minutes from where we lived, so it gave me an extended time in the car with Lynn to ply my persuasive powers on her. After I convinced her to at least drive up and meet this dog, we arranged to head out on a Saturday morning.

I wish I could tell you my degree in communications made the difference on that drive. I wish I could tell you that my persuasive speaking abilities paid off in a big way. I wish I could tell you my powerful logic won Lynn over. I wish I could tell you I clearly wore the pants in the family that day! Unfortunately, none of that proved to be true during our drive to north Phoenix that day. We arrived at Alex's foster home with Lynn as dead-set against a big dog as she was when we started the trip.

I was crushed.

As Alex's foster owners ushered us into their family room, I took a corner on the couch, trying to put a game face on what was undoubtedly a wasted trip.

Lynn told me later that, at the same time as I was moping, she began to notice what a beautiful home we were in. These owners of two Goldens, and now foster parents of a third, had beautiful white carpet; we were sitting on a beautiful white couch, and had crossed over a clean and tidy tile floor to get there. This is not the kind of house she had imagined a big, impolite, dirty dog would live in.

After visiting for a few minutes, Alex was brought in. What a beautiful dog! Big, red, happy eyes and a wagging tail, he walked into the room like a prince among dogs. This was the dog I had hoped for, a dog to wrestle with, a dog to run with, a dog to take to a tailgate party! Too bad he wasn't going to be our dog. Too bad my persuasive powers had failed on the trip north. Too bad Alex would be passed over in favor of some small, "harmless" dog.

I was more than crushed. I was devastated. The perfect dog. So close, yet so far. All because Lynn was opposed to getting a big dog.

While all this was racing through my mind, Alex walked toward the white couch where Lynn and I were seated. Slowly. Politely. Gracefully. Upon reaching the couch, Alex sat down on the floor quietly next to her, and ignoring me almost completely, gently put his paw on the couch next to her as if to say, "It is a pleasure to meet you." The perfect gentleman.

At that point, all Lynn's objections evaporated. Alex and Lynn connected, and Alex became our first rescued Golden and a wonderful addition to our family. Big and happy, he wrestled with me on the family room floor and went on runs with both of us. He took trips to Home Depot and showed up on the sidelines for pick-up football games. He slept beside our bed, welcomed Kaibab, our second Golden, as his companion when she joined our family, and he never once stuck his nose in impolite places.

Alex also demonstrated an uncanny knack for reading people. I don't care what others think; he made me a believer in a dog's sixth sense. In fact, his ability to "zero-in" on Lynn and woo her at that very first meeting was a clear demonstration that he knew what all wise leaders learn, the fourth principle in this book:

Always know who your most important audience is.

Alex knew whom he needed to reach. His uncanny ability to read the situation and see who needed convincing worked in his favor – and mine.

s every father of a teenage daughter does, I've been dreading the day that I knew would eventually come. Boys!

I was hoping they wouldn't notice Drew until she was 25 or 30. Unfortunately, I married a beautiful woman, and Drew inherited her mom's good looks. Boys were interested long before I was prepared - like 10 or 20 years before I was prepared!

Shortly after boys started showing up, one or two of them started to become more serious. Boys were transforming them-selves into boyfriends. This was an issue. An issue that needed to be dealt with.

Not having gone down this path before, we approached it like we approach many issues in our family. We had a family meeting. Lynn, Drew and I sat down and talked about this new reality and how we were going to deal with it. My humorous suggestion to deal with this issue with guns and knives was dismissed without any laughter on Drew's part (okay, she at least rolled her eyes -

I think she kind of enjoys that I threaten to eliminate every teenage boy that lives within 400 miles of our house). After a considerable amount of conversation, we arrived at several "ground rules" that we all could live with.

One of our ground rules is this: every time a boy arrives at our house to take Drew on a date, he and I spend a few minutes in the family room. I ask him some hard questions about respect and honor, and I talk very clearly to him about how precious Drew is to her mom and me. The whole time we are talking, I make sure my voice is just loud enough that Drew, who is in her bedroom right above the railing overlooking our family room, can hear what I say. I want her to hear me talk with him. I want her to hear how I love her and expect this boy to treat her with respect and honor. I want her to know that I've had a very straightforward conversation with him and am holding him accountable for his actions.

I may be talking to this boy, but, in many respects, my most important audience is Drew, who knows that her dad takes his role as her father very seriously.

This is an insight that good leaders always seem to understand. Know who you really need to communicate with. From the CEO who uses the quarterly analyst call to communicate to shareholders the future direction of the company to the sales professional who speaks the language of her prospect's economic decision-maker when responding to a Request-for-Proposal. From the camp counselor who talks to the frightened new junior campers while really reassuring their parents that the children will be safe to the politician who uses her speeches on the floor of Congress to really reach her constituents back home, wise leaders always know who they really need to communicate with.

A manager I was interviewing recently said he always sends internal emails about his subordinates to his superior, written in such a way that they will get back to his subordinates, sending them messages that he wants them to hear. He understands who his most important audience is, and makes sure he communicates so that they get it.

A retail manager I worked with several years ago arranged his back-office in such a way that customers coming in the front of the store could see him and he could see them. His real purpose was to let his employees know how open they all were to be with their customers.

We live in Austin, Texas, home of the University of Texas. The Longhorns are a perennial top-ten collegiate football team. Coach Mac Brown has won more than 100 games in his first ten years coaching them, including one national championship.

The Longhorns dominate the local paper's sports section, and Coach Brown is interviewed regularly. Recently I read an article where he was talking about the upcoming season. In the interview, he emphasized to the reporter that virtually none of the 22 starting positions on the football field had been won by any specific players. Players were still competing hard to earn the right to step out on the field and represent the university in the season-opening game a few weeks away. He made it very clear to this reporter that each player needed to work very diligently in the upcoming practice sessions to earn that starting position. As I finished the article, it occurred to me that his message was not primarily for the reporter or even the reading audience across Austin – the many loyal football fans that scan the sports section every day for information on the upcoming season.

Coach Brown's real audience that day was his players. He used his newspaper interview to communicate to each one of them. Work hard. Every day. Every practice. Every play. Don't assume anything. Earn the right to become a starter.

June 18, 1940 was a dark day in Western Europe. Barely more than a month before, Germany began a massive attack against France, Holland, Belgium and Luxembourg that proved to be the last battle before Germany turned all its might on the island of England. Although relatively evenly matched by the French and European defenders, German's modern war capabilities quickly overpowered the defenders. By mid-June, all that separated Germany from total domination of Europe was the English Channel and a weakening Royal Air Force. At that point, British Prime Minister Winston Churchill took to the airwaves to speak to the English people.

Churchill's speech, familiarly known as the "Finest Hour" speech, was delivered before Great Britain's House of Commons. But his speech wasn't really for the House of Commons. Here's a transcript of the final ninety seconds of his speech:

> *"What General Weygand called the Battle of France is over. I expect that the Battle of Britain is about to begin. Upon this battle depends the survival of Christian civilization. Upon it depends our own British life, and the long continuity of our institutions and our Empire. The whole fury and might of the enemy must very soon be turned on us.*

> *"Hitler knows that he will have to break us in this Island or lose the war. If we can stand up to him, all Europe may be free and the life of the world may*

*move forward into broad, sunlit uplands. But if we
fail, then the whole world, including the United
States, including all that we have known and cared
for, will sink into the abyss of a new Dark Age made
more sinister, and perhaps more protracted, by the
lights of perverted science.*

*"Let us therefore brace ourselves to our duties, and
so bear ourselves that if the British Empire and its
Commonwealth last for a thousand years, men will
still say, 'This was their finest hour.'"*

This was truly an inspiring speech. But who was Churchill's
real intended audience? I believe he had three specific audiences in
mind.

First and foremost, he was speaking to the pilots in the Royal
Air Force. This rag-tag band of young, inexperienced flyers was
being asked to do the impossible: hold off the military might of a
vastly more superior air power as German fighter planes and
bombers repeatedly crossed the English Channel to attack England.
His speech was a call to them to rise to this great crisis and per-
form heroic acts, which they did.

Secondly, Churchill was speaking to the common people of
England, who were being subject to relentless nightly bombing
raids and needed the courage to continue.

His third, and perhaps most important audience, was the United
States, which hadn't yet joined the war effort. In fact, many people
in the United States remained strongly opposed to American par-
ticipation in the war. So Churchill was purposeful in his speech,
communicating to the people across the Atlantic that this war was
also their war.

By knowing who his real audience was, Churchill was able to communicate to the British House of Commons while really communicating to those he mostly sought to influence.

One other famous leader demonstrated this principle of knowing who your most important audience was. At least a leader that is famous to my family.

Miss Gavin was my daughter's second grade teacher. We had just moved to Austin, and Drew was in a new school. Her mom and I were a bit anxious about her fitting in with new children in a new environment, but knew she was a well-balanced, outgoing child, and hoped she would connect early on with some other girls. So we were pleased when Drew seemed to befriend one particular girl early on and relatively quickly had a new "best friend."

Our first parent-teacher-student meeting happened six weeks into the school year. At the meeting, Miss Gavin spoke positively with us about Drew's academic abilities. Drew sat to the side and listened politely, showing us the different school assignments she had worked on.

Toward the end of our meeting, Miss Gavin said there was one other topic she wanted to bring up with the two of us. She then carefully and wisely told us that there was one mean girl in class, and that Drew, because of her desire to fit in, had allowed herself to be befriended by this girl, and was starting to say mean things herself to some of the other kids in the class. Miss Gavin's words were kind but firm, gracious and caring, and while they were addressed to us, the parents, were really intended to be heard by the ears of an eager-to-please, tender-hearted second-grader.

I will never forget what happened next. Drew, seven years old, burst into tears, reached up to the arms of her second-grade teacher, and was cradled in the lap of this wise-beyond-her-years lady who reached out to her. "I'm sorry," was all we could hear at first as Drew sobbed into the shoulder of this wonderful lady.

Drew knew she had been mean to several of her classmates, and didn't want it to continue, but didn't know how to stop, since she was "best friends" with this other girl.

Fifteen minutes later, tears on the part of parents, teacher and student alike, we all agreed that Drew's heart never intended to be mean, but she needed to do a better job of standing up for what she knew was right and not be so eager to please one friend.

Then the four of us strategized together on ways Drew could be friends with all the children in the class. In the next several weeks, Drew slowly moved away from the mean girl and found several other new "best friends" who shared her tender heart and kindness.

That parent-teacher-student meeting was years ago now, but I've never forgotten it. Miss Gavin demonstrated to me that night her wisdom when she used words addressed to us as parents, to really speak to the heart of our daughter.

I will always be grateful for a woman who knew who her real audience was.

LEADERSHIP APPLICATION

Golden Principle Number Four
Always know who your most important audience is.

1. *Who do you know who does a good job of applying this principle in their communication?*

2. *What two or three specific things do they do to demonstrate this principle?*

3. *What challenges do you face in practicing this principle?*

4. *What two or three specific things can you begin doing in order to reach who you really need to reach?*

Golden Principle Number Five

Emotional commitment comes
through emotional connection.

I'm the cat guy. I don't like being the cat guy, but I am.

Redford and Rascal are best friends. They play together, bask in the sun on our back porch together, sleep together, even share food at times. Apparently neither one of them read the fine print in their respective animal contracts, which states they are supposed to be mortal enemies. Redford the dog loves Rascal the cat. And vice versa.

All of our animals have been rescued. Some, like Redford, were rescued from bad situations. Most of the others were taken from situations where they were at least neglected: neighbors who were moving, animals that got lost, kids going off to college, and so on. Rascal's story is different.

It was a late night one spring several years ago. Lynn and I decided to take the dogs for a walk. Our neighborhood is quite hilly and heavily wooded, with a number of greenbelts and open spaces between houses. We had just crested the top of the hill a few blocks from our house when another late-night walker alerted us to "some type of wild animal" a block or so away that was making a "horribly terrifying sound."

"You don't want to go down that street," he said as he quickly walked the other direction.

As soon as he said that, Lynn knew my adventuresome spirit would require us to go down that exact street, which we promptly did, with the dogs walking alongside.

And indeed, when we got to the end of the street, we did hear a very unusual sound – not "horrible" and "terrifying," but definitely animal in nature. We narrowed down where the sound was coming from, and after looking through some bushes in a front yard, we found the sound-originator: a very tiny 4- or 5-week old kitten, trying to get in the window of house and yelling at the top of his lungs, making a very large sound for such a small body.

The sound this tiny cat was making was not a meow or a hiss, but somewhere in between, and much louder than such a small animal should be capable of. We were concerned for him, and knocked on the door of the house where he was hiding. The people who answered told us that it wasn't their kitten, but they had been disturbed by the noise for quite some time. Several other houses elicited the same response.

We ultimately assumed the kitten must have been born in the woods adjacent to one of these houses, was starving, and had come out into the neighborhood to beg for food. Being the animal people we are, we intended to pick it up, take it home overnight and drop it off at the animal shelter the next day. However, the cat had a different idea.

Each time I tried to pick up the kitten, it found a way to squeeze through my fingers and jump to the ground to walk with the dogs, until finally I gave up and let it walk with us. We must have made quite a sight: 2 large Goldens walking down the street with one very small, starving kitten weaving weakly between their legs.

This went on for almost a mile until we got back to the house, where Drew was waiting up. As soon as she saw the kitten, she announced, "You are not taking the kitten to the animal shelter. His name is Rascal, and he belongs with us."

And so Rascal became part of our family.

And Rascal also became an on-going embarrassment for me. You see, in my family, I'm the *cat guy*. Let me make it very clear: I don't want to be the cat guy. I picture myself as more of a Golden Retriever guy or a Labrador guy. Even a German Shepherd guy. Some big, strong, outgoing, humble-but-popular type of dog (undoubtedly tied to some ongoing deep-rooted personal psychosis) I'm not a small-dog guy. And definitely not a cat guy. Unfortunately, Rascal has a different opinion. He thinks we share a lot in common.

For instance, because of my travels, I'm gone a lot, just like the cat. Rascal is an indoor-outdoor cat who uses the doggie door to come and go as he pleases.

I often get home late at night, just like the cat.

I'm the only man in the house. Rascal is the only cat in the house.

I think I'm outgoing and pleasant, but I've been told more than once by my family members that I can appear aloof and disinterested – these are characteristics that Rascal has honed to a fine art.

And so Rascal identifies with me.

In fact, it is a regular occasion that as I am pulling into the driveway late at night, while the dogs are sleeping ignorantly inside, Rascal comes running down the street to greet me. Who knows where he has been – out carousing with other neighborhood cats, I suspect. All I know is that he comes running when I get home. Because he identifies with me, he is connected to me. I wish he wasn't, but he is.

On the other hand, Redford and Sammi are glad to see me, but they are also very comfortable being home with my family when I travel. I like to think they miss me, but I'm not entirely sure they do.

The dogs love Lynn the best. A large part of her work is executive coaching by phone, and she works out of our den. When she is working, Redford usually stays in the space under her desk so that he can be near her.

All day long Lynn, almost unconsciously, pets Redford with her feet. She's busy working but Redford feels her touch, and, as a result, feels connected to her. She is Redford's favorite because she spends so much time with him. As a result, if you give Redford a choice of whom he wants to be with, he always chooses Lynn.

Even when I'm home, if I'm in the kitchen or family room and Lynn is in the den, Redford may come out to say hello to me, but then he promptly heads back to be near Lynn.

When we are in the backyard, you will invariably find Redford close to Lynn.

At mealtime, Redford won't eat if I'm near his bowl (we suspect he may have been teased or even abused at mealtime at the puppy mill). But he has no problem eating with Lynn around.

When we walk the dogs through the neighborhood, Redford much prefers to have his leash held by Lynn.

It isn't that he doesn't like me – he likes me a lot. He's just "connected" to Lynn.

As a cat, Rascal doesn't need much affection. In fact, the poorer I treat him, the more he connects with me. Don't ask me why – it's a cat thing.

On the other hand, because Lynn spends so much time with Redford, he has a very strong bond with her. And as a result, he listens to her more closely, responds to her better and is more obedient to her than me.

But this Golden principle is not just about Redford. It is about families. It is about friendships. It is about work relationships. It is about any relationships where you need commitment:

Emotional commitment comes from emotional connection.

There is a well-known article from the *Harvard Business Review* many years ago that captures the power of emotional commitment in a business setting. One company became an acquisition target for a much larger company, but in order for the acquisition to meet strict financial criteria, the owner of the smaller firm was told to lay-off a significant portion of his workforce. Many people were going to lose their jobs – not for poor performance or as a result of poor reviews, but only due to the acquiring company's fiscal requirements. While a very difficult task to implement, the president of the target company chose to meet personally with everyone who was being dismissed, to be able to look them face-to-face and eye-to-eye, to explain the difficult decision that was made. These meetings took place over a number of days, and they were very difficult meetings. There were many angry employees - the president was accused of selling out, he was yelled at and threatened.

The easy thing for that president to do would have been to avoid the face-to-face meetings. But he knew his employees deserved his emotional commitment.

The good news was that the acquisition took place, and shortly into the new arrangement, this small company, which was now a subsidiary of the larger parent company, did very well. So well, in fact, the parent company decided to increase capitalization, ramp up production and grow this subsidiary. So the president of this subsidiary was given the commission to add staffing and production capacity in order to grow this line of business.

Here's the powerful reality of Golden Principle #5: when the president of this new subsidiary contacted his former employees to see if they would be interested in leaving their new jobs to return to work for him, many did so – even though he had fired them literally months before! Because they knew of his *emotional connection* to them, as demonstrated in his face-to-face meetings with them when they were laid off, they had a tremendous sense of *emotional commitment* to him.

S am Russell was another leader who understood Golden Principle Number Five. Sam was my very first sales manager. She was one of the owners of a small real estate firm in Phoenix in the 1980s. I was teaching at a local high school and had summers off, so I got my real estate license and worked for Sam's firm for a couple of summers.

I'll never forget my first summer sitting open houses. I actually had some good success, and had a number of contracts pending when I went back to school that fall. Here's the problem: while I had "sold" several houses, none of them had closed yet, and I had no clue what I was doing; I was sure every one of the deals was going to blow up and have all sorts of problems. So I apologized to Sam as I turned the contracts over to her, explaining that while I had enjoyed my new work, I wasn't very good yet because I had so much to learn.

After she assured me that I would be very successful in real estate if I ever chose to do it full-time, she told me I would be good because I already understood sales rule #1:

People don't care how much you know
until they know how much you care -
people buy from people they like.

In many respects, Sam's sales rule #1 is simply a business application of Golden Principle #5. People make buying decisions to a great degree based on how they feel about the salesperson they are working with. Their commitment to spend money on your product or service is directly tied to the connection you establish with them.

The best leaders are *people* people. You can't get their heads unless you get their hearts. Every effective leader knows this truth, and appeals to emotions as well as intellect.

T he movie *Rudy* that came out in 1993, was based on the true story of Rudy Ruettiger, an undersized-but-overachieving football player for Notre Dame University. Rudy Ruettiger came from a struggling blue-collar family, but chose to follow his dream and go to college. His aspirations were not just for any college, however; his goal was to attend the pinnacle of academics and athletics: Notre Dame.

Unfortunately, Rudy's high school grades were not good enough to allow for admittance to Notre Dame, so he did the next best thing and left home to go to Holy Cross Junior College for two years. Holy Cross is located across the street from Notre Dame, allowing Rudy to keep his vision alive: he could see Notre Dame every day and spend a lot of time on that hallowed campus.

Rudy had to work very hard at Holy Cross for those two years in order to pull his grades up to admission levels at Notre Dame; in fact, it was during his time at Holy Cross that Rudy was diagnosed with the reading disorder *Dyslexia*. In order to maintain a "B" average – the minimum it would take to get in to Notre Dame - he really had to learn how to study. With the help of his teachers and tutors he was able to focus on his grades and get the job done. And after three rejections from Notre Dame, his dream to attend this prestigious university finally came true.

Rudy transferred to Notre Dame in the fall of 1974. While at Notre Dame, Rudy attempted to live out another dream: to play football for the *Fighting Irish*. Rudy walked on the team under the coaching staff of Ara Parseghian in 1974. Despite the fact that he was significantly smaller and slower than any of the scholarship athletes, he worked his guts out and treated every practice like it was a real game, which was good because that is all that Rudy ever got to do – for three years in a row he practiced every day, often being used as part of the "scout team" and being run roughshod over by some of Notre Dame's finest varsity athletes. But he never got to even "suit-up" for a real game.

Rudy never quit, and he slowly won the respect and emotional commitment of his teammates because of his hard work and intensity at practice. In fact, he won their respect so thoroughly that the movie portrays a scene at the end of his senior season where his team members refuse to play without Rudy in the last game of his senior year. One by one, they walk into the coach's office and lay down their jerseys, informing the coach that they wouldn't play if Rudy didn't. He had earned their emotional commitment.

Rudy, Redford and Rascal. All of them demonstrate the power of this principle: Emotional Commitment comes through Emotional Connection. This is a lesson that all leaders need to learn, and one that wise leaders learn to practice.

Postscript:

Several months before this book went to press, Rascal disappeared. He didn't come home one night. We looked for him for hours. We put up signs in the neighborhood. We contacted local vets and the animal shelter, but all to no avail. We've since learned that the life expectancy for indoor-outdoor cats is five years, which was how old Rascal was. We don't know what happened to Rascal, and are afraid to think about it. While doubtful, we are hoping he was taken home by some other family.

Several months later, Nicolas showed up. Another feral kitten, he attached himself to Drew while she was out front on Christmas Eve. One week and $800 later, "Nicholas" the Christmas cat was spayed, vaccinated and given a clean bill of health by our vet. We learned our lesson with Rascal – Nicholas has become an inside cat.

One other thing – despite my best efforts, Nicholas likes me best.

LEADERSHIP APPLICATION

Golden Principle Number Five

Emotional commitment comes through emotional connection.

1. *What leader do you know who does a good job of applying this principle?*

2. *What two or three specific things do they do to live out this principle?*

3. *What challenges do you face in living out this principle?*

4. *What two or three specific things can you begin doing in order to better live out this principle?*

Golden Principle Number Six

Leading – and loving – are always
expensive propositions.

"Free dogs" is an oxymoron.

S eventeen hundred fifty dollars. The week before Christmas.

Not a great time to incur a significant un-planned expense.

Sammi stopped eating eight days before Christmas. Two days later we were at the vet. Four hundred dollars, and a series of diagnostic tests later, we were sent home with the dog, a slew of medications and an unclear prognosis. The vet couldn't find anything wrong.

That night Sammi threw up the remains of a chewed-up ball. We thought the culprit was identified. Twenty-four hours later she still wasn't eating. Another trip to the vet.

Thirteen hundred and fifty dollars later, major stomach surgery and a second slew of medications did the trick. She started eating again.

We were left emotionally relieved and $1750.00 poorer.

Dogs are expensive.

I n the last twenty years, we've adopted eight dogs and three cats. We didn't buy any of them, but they definitely weren't free. I suspect we've spent more than $20,000 on their healthcare. And that doesn't include food, snacks, training, boarding, licensing, carpet-cleaning, chewed baseboard-repairing, crate-purchasing, indoor barricade-building and outdoor fence-erecting (along with replacing several pairs of Lynn's and Drew's favorite shoes!)

Are the dogs worth it? Without a doubt.

That leads us to Golden Principle number six:

Leading – and loving- are always expensive propositions.

The first couple of years, we were surprised by how much our "free" dogs cost us. Alex, our first Golden, and Kaibab, his comrade-in-arms, both had expensive health issues. And it wasn't just the dogs. Our cats have drained our savings account at well. Ironically, the only pet we ever purchased, Buddy the Cockatiel, has cost us the least.

While the reality of Golden Principle number six has hit us financially, the most important demonstration of this principle often doesn't have to do primarily with money. It has to do with other things. Time. Heartache. Disappointment. All expensive propositions.

When we lost Alex, we were devastated. I was out of town at the time, and Lynn called to let me know he had passed away. In the midst of my tears, a wise friend shared with me two thoughts.

First of all, whether we recognized it or not, the day we adopted our first pet, we made a unwritten covenant with that sweet animal that we would grieve at it's passing.

The truth is, unless you raise tortoises or macaws, your life expectancy is longer than your pets. You will outlive them, and your heart will be broken when they pass away. My wise friend helped me understand that part of our love for our pets was the recognition that we would bury our pets; it is the gift we give them to help them pass away knowing they have been loved. Loving them is wonderful; it is also emotionally expensive.

Secondly, my wise friend shared with me an interesting thought he read in one of C.S. Lewis's writings. C.S. Lewis was a deeply devout Christian and studied the scriptures earnestly. In Lewis' studies, he came to recognize that heaven is a place where all our love will be complete, and a place of perfect fulfillment.

In his logic, therefore, since our pets give us great love and fulfillment, they go before us to wait for us in heaven - our pets will be with us in the afterlife. I've never been able to find the C.S. Lewis illustration my friend referred to, but I cling to it with hope. Alex, Kaibab, Jody, Trooper, Ranger, Smokey and Rascal are waiting for us. It may be a silly hope, but for those of us who love pets, we know what hope that offers.

Nevertheless, while we live and see our pets grow old before our eyes, we realize this very profound principle that loving them is going to be an expensive proposition.

This principle goes far beyond pets, however. It applies to every intimate relationship.

Lynn and I have been married for more that 25 years. I married my college sweetheart, and was one of the fortunate ones to *marry up*.

And even though we continue to love each other deeply, we also hurt each other at times. Neither one of us is perfect, and because of the closeness of our relationship – the love we share with each other – our imperfections hurt each other. Those cute little idiosyncrasies that were endearing when we were dating slowly stopped being cute little idiosyncrasies. After a while, they became small annoyances. As more time went on, those small annoyances grew. Over time, some of them have turned into fingernails-on-a-chalkboard! Like my memory.

I have a poor memory. Not a terrible memory, but a poor one. I don't miss things like anniversaries and birthdays, but I forget to go to the grocery store on the way home, meaning Lynn has to run out before dinner to get meal ingredients. I forget to take my wallet to the airport, meaning Lynn has to race there to meet me at the curb, my wallet in her hand, so I don't miss my flight. The list goes on, but I think you get my point.

A number of years ago, I got in an accident while driving her car. Nothing serious, but it required us to have the car in the shop. And so we borrowed a vehicle from Lynn's dad: a 1979 hunter's special full-size Ford pick-up. A real truck! The kind with the gun rack in the back window and the guy with chewing tobacco driving. Not the kind Lynn would see us having. But that was okay, since I drove it most of the time while her car was being fixed. Except one morning.

I had an early morning meeting where I was picking up a business client, and needed our nice car. So I left the truck for Lynn.

She was in a hurry that morning, trying to get infant Drew up and to the baby-sitter while getting ready for an important meeting with another business client to which she was going to be forced to drive the truck. Except for one minor detail - I forgot to leave the truck key for her. So here she was, crying baby in her arms, business outfit increasingly disheveled, late for an important meeting, and no key! Ouch! Furthermore, I forgot to turn on my pager that morning - she wasn't even able to get a message to me. OUCH!

My poor memory caused Lynn incredible frustration that morning, as it has any number of times throughout our marriage. And she has had to learn to live with my shortcoming in this area. Does she enjoy it? No. Does this give me permission to never work on improving my memory? No way. Nevertheless, Lynn has to live with this shortcoming of mine. Living with it is helping to make her a more patient person. But it is still expensive.

As I think of the reality Lynn has lived with for more than 25 years, I'm reminded of a quote by Sam Levenson:

"Love at first sight is easy to understand.
It's when two people have been looking at each other
for years that it becomes a miracle."

Loving is always an expensive proposition.

T his principle isn't just true for loving relationships. It is also true regarding leadership.

1. Expect to be disappointed

A number of years ago, I was a new leader in a growing non-profit. We counted on volunteers to invest time, energy and finances for our mission to be advanced. After I experienced a number of disappointments and set-backs due to volunteers who failed to keep their commitments, I was approached by a senior leader in our organization. He shared with me a principle I have never forgotten: "If you are going to be in a leadership position, expect to be disappointed." His point was one of several fundamental applications of Golden Principle number six.

2. Expect to be held to a higher standard

Leaders are examined more closely and held to higher expectations. As I write this chapter, the newspapers are filled with information on the various presidential candidates running for office in 2008. Can you imagine the magnifying glass they live their lives under? Seemingly everything they've ever done is discussed and dissected *ad nauseum*. Is it fair? Probably not. However, while I'm no fan of yellow journalism, to a certain extent we are justified in holding our leaders to a higher standard. As soon and you and I assume the mantle of leadership, we tacitly agreed to a contract with those we influence that our lives will model and reflect the principles we espouse to those under us.

I have a problem with many airline pilots. Perhaps it is just that I'm mistaken in my assumption that the pilots at the front of commercial flights are leaders. Maybe I need to remember that in some respects they are just bus drivers.

Here's the type of thing that bothers me: recently I was flying to Columbus, Ohio on a small regional jet. Before we boarded the flight, the gate attendant informed us that the plane was "weight-limited" (too many passengers with too many suitcases) and they needed four volunteers to miss this flight and take a later flight. They offered a discount coupon on future flights to anyone who volunteered. No one budged - we all needed to get to Columbus on time.

Ten minutes later, the gate attendant repeated the announcement, and also informed us – in a somewhat belittling manner - that we would all be delayed until four people volunteered. Again no one budged. Five minutes later the same announcement, the same belittling tone. Finally some volunteers agreed to wait, and the rest of us boarded the plane.

The frustration of this weight-limit issue was that I saw one of the pilots get on the plane a few minutes prior to the announcements. He was carrying 4 suitcases, including a guitar, and stored all of them in the front closet of the airplane, severely limiting the amount of storage space for passengers. I see this type of behavior happen regularly: flight attendants who bring multiple suitcases on airplanes, pilots and flight attendants who store their bags in the initial overhead bins, requiring the first row or two of passengers to find other places to store their suitcases, and so on. Perhaps this is just a little thing, but I find myself very annoyed. If the guitar-toting pilot were truly a leader, his self-sacrifice would model for all of us his desire to lead us well.

I guess I just needed to remember: he wasn't a leader, he was just a bus driver. The reminder I took away:

Leadership is less about position,
and more about responsibility.

S ometimes this principle of higher accountability is much more significant than simply not enough storage space on airplanes. Sometimes it ends up costing you your job. Sometimes it can even lead to legal impact.

We lived in Phoenix throughout the 1990s. Bill Crotts was a business acquaintance of mine at that time. I did some consulting and writing for the firm he headed up, the Baptist Foundation of Arizona. That made the spring of 2007 a particularly sad one for me. Based on a judge's ruling early in the year, Bill Crotts headed off to prison. His crime? Heading up a "Ponzi Scheme" that cost investors in the BFA an estimated $550 million dollars.

The cost of the loss was so large that it drove the consulting firm Arthur Anderson out of business. As the testimony came out during the last months and years, the BFA apparently used newer deposits to pay off older depositors while hiding losses off the books. A classic house of cards that came crashing down several years ago, leaving many investors destitute.

According to the judge, in addition to his eight-year prison term, Bill will be required to pay $159 million in restitution to the victims. Here's the problem with that: Bill doesn't have the money.

In fact, as far as anyone can tell, Bill never financially benefited from this Ponzi scheme. Bill is not an evil man, and he wasn't bent on bilking investors, many of whom were elderly retirees, of their life savings. What really was Bill's crime? It was one that every leader needs to be diligent to avoid. It was an issue of competence.

At some point, things spun out of control. Leading a multi-million-dollar financial institution required incredible effort and diligence. Whether Bill and his leadership team weren't up to the task or whether they decided to not do the hard work required to keep the finances in order, their lack of competence on behalf of their investors caused many to lose their life savings.

T o be perfectly honest, I wish leadership competence wasn't such a big deal. Other aspects of leadership fire me up more. Thinking about the power of a leader's moral character or the inspiration of a leader's calling gives me a great deal of energy. Recognizing that a leader must also work tremendously hard to be diligent and competent scares me. Am I willing to pay the price to lead? Will I do the hard work of preparing myself to lead? Can I pay the price of hard effort — sweat-of-the-brow kind of effort — to lead?

Leaders can't just *mean well*. Competence counts. As my wise mother-in-law used to say, "Good intentions never did anyone any good." As trustworthy leaders, we need to do our work with excellence and diligence.

That's another one of the implications of Golden Principle number six.

There is a cost – in sweat and blood – of leading well.

L ynn called me while I was on the road this week. Redford got in our closet and chewed one of her shoes. Not a worn out running shoe or a cheap sandal. A dress shoe - one of her favorites. Made by Coach. A high-end, costly shoe.

We are heading to the store this weekend to see about a replacement pair.

Leadership is expensive.

LEADERSHIP APPLICATION

Golden Principle Number Six

Leading – and loving – are always expensive propositions.

1. What leader do you know who does a good job of applying this principle?

2. What two or three specific things do they do to live out this principle?

3. What challenges do you face in living out this principle?

4. What two or three specific things can you begin doing in order to better live out this principle?

Golden Principle Number Seven

It's not about me.

The "I" word…

Sammi started limping after our 3-mile run one afternoon about two years ago. Sammi has been a great running partner over the years, but she is starting to get a little older, and I didn't think anything of it. We thought maybe she just needed to run once or twice a week instead of three times.

Unfortunately, the limp didn't go away. It would come and go – some days and some runs she was fine, but other days she limped all day long. Eventually we knew we needed to get it checked out. Several vet trips and specialist exams later, we found out that Sammi had a slow growing cancer in the bone in her front left leg. After discussing our options, we had Sammi go in for surgery, and the tumor was removed. Unfortunately, the doctors warned us of the possibility, and indeed the cancer has slowly come back. Sammi is limping again. All the time. And she is licking her front leg a lot – a sign that it pains her.

We need to do something. The bad news is that because of the tumor's location, if they do surgery again, she will lose her leg.

And so we find ourselves grieving over Sammi losing her leg. We know we will need to move forward at some point, and sooner rather than later. But how will she cope? She is so energetic and fun-loving. Always ready for a party. Always ready for a wrestling match. Always ready to chase the ball. And despite her age, she is still able to out-hustle and out-smart our younger dogs. If she lost her leg, it would devastate her. And us.

Julie Smith is a veterinarian in Colorado and a long-time family friend. Recently Lynn was on the phone with Julie, grieving over Sammi's leg. Julie's response surprised both of us.

She said, "Dogs aren't like people. They don't have egos or get embarrassed or worry about what people are thinking about them. Sammi will adapt and not think about the handicap. She won't grieve the loss. She will live in the moment."

And then Julie reminded us about Gracie. Like so many vets, Julie Smith didn't go into veterinary medicine for the money. In fact, being a vet is Julie's second career. In her 40s she returned to college to get her vet degree because of her great love for animals. Whether hutch bunnies, feral cats, handicapped dogs or aging horses, Julie loves to take care of animals.

In his excellent book, *Now Discover Your Strengths*, Marcus Buckingham shares the unfortunate statistic that only twenty percent of business people surveyed in a large Gallup poll said they get to do what they are best at for their work. While she didn't participate in this large Gallup pole, undoubtedly Julie would be one of the twenty percent. She was born to care for animals. And she understands them well. Her comments to us about Sammi coping with the loss of her leg was based on her firsthand knowledge from working with lots of handicapped pets, and also based on experiences with her own dog, Gracie.

Gracie was a spotted spaniel that Julie adopted a number of years ago. Her name fit her personality. Gracie was gracious and warm. If she appeared a bit reserved, it was only because she didn't want to bowl you over. Gracie quickly became more than just a pet. In fact, Gracie went with Dr. Julie to Julie's vet clinic every day for years, padding the hallways, greeting newcomers, calming other animals as they arrived, and mainly hanging out under Julie's desk. They were fast friends. And over time, Gracie got old. At one point, Gracie had a mild stroke. Fortunately for her, Dr. Julie was there to care for her. Then Gracie's hips started to fail. She would lie down, but couldn't get back up. The cold bothered her. And she couldn't make it up the steps in Julie's house to the bedroom at night. Gracie wasn't in any pain, but she was losing her mobility.

What did Dr. Julie do? She got Gracie a "helper harness." This harness was a couple of straps that went under Gracie's body, with a handle on top. When it was time to go upstairs, Julie simply used the harness to help Gracie up. In and out of the car? No problem. Getting around the vet clinic – with Julie's harness, Gracie did just fine. Did Gracie mind the harness? Was she embarrassed to be at the vet clinic, among all the other animals, with a contraption attached to her back? Did she growl at Julie when Julie put the harness on? Never. She simply lived in the moment, not focusing on her infirmities, but on the world around her.

It's not about me.

There is a powerful leadership lesson here. As leaders, and as people, I'm convinced most of us worry about what people think about us far too much of the time. Dogs, on the other hand, don't care. As long as Gracie is loved by Julie, she doesn't think about herself.

That's just the problem for many leaders: we mistakenly think it is all about us. We make our position of supreme importance. We protect our turf. We get indignant when we are ignored. And as a result, our influence is diminished.

One hundred and twenty-five and counting. It was like fingernails on a chalkboard.

I was attending a training workshop recently, and the leader used "I" more than should have been humanly possible in four hours. I stopped counting at 125. Unfortunately, he kept right on going.

"I am going to teach you."

"Let me tell you what I think."

"I know you will benefit from this."

"I have an opinion about that . . ."

"I don't mean to disagree with you, but . . ."

In addition to the blatant use of the "I" word, he made sure he shared several examples from his own background that showed how smart and successful he had been.

Rather than leading a successful adult-learning experience, where the participants worked together to gain new understanding and application, he told them what to do. And I saw many participants sitting back with their arms crossed as if to say: "I'm not buying what you are selling."

However, he was so into "I" that he couldn't recognize their indifference. In fact, when a couple of them pushed back, it was very evident from his comments that he thought they were the ones with the problems - not him.

Sometimes our best mentors are "anti-mentors" – people who show us what not to do. I definitely learned a lesson that day. In effective leadership, there is very little room for the "I" word.

My experience with the "I" leader was in marked contrast to Helen Sutton's approach. Helen is a Senior Training Consultant for Richardson, a leading international provider of sales and sales management training and consulting, and a co-worker of mine. Helen leads workshops for business and sales professionals more than one hundred days a year all over the world, working with some of the leading Fortune 500 companies here and abroad.

In just about every workshop Helen leads, whether it is for sales professionals or business leaders, she finds a way to create a flip-chart early in the day with just four words on it. Written large in bold ink, these four words capture Helen's conviction about effective selling and effective leadership.

Her four words? The very same words that define this Golden Principle: "Its Not About Me."

Helen Sutton is convinced one of the most important lessons she needs to make sure her workshop participants get is this: if you want to be more effective in sales, if you want to be a better business leader – if you want to be a better person - you've got to get over yourself. It can't be about you.

The word *anthropocentrism* is a combination of a couple of Latin cognates. *Anthropo-* having to do with the study of man and *-centrism* meaning the center of focus. One aspect of anthropocentrism is *self-centrism*. It is me, wanting you to notice me. It is me positioning myself so that I look good. It is me making sure that the credit comes back to me.

I've gotten pretty good over the years at appearing to be subtle. I can "play the humility game" pretty well. But when I am at my worst, I can be pretty petty. I want to win. I want to look good. I want all the marbles. I want you to envy me. I end up believing my own messages, and expect you to do the same. Self-centrism ends up being a very ugly thing.

The best business leaders understand this, and work very hard to listen to those whom they influence.

W here do you find yourself? How much does "I" play a role in your attempts at influence, and within your relationships?

Pope John Paul was a great man, a great leader and one of the greatest Popes in the history of the Catholic Church. A tough act to follow. Cardinal Joseph Ratzinger knew that. When he was named to succeed John Paul as Pope after a surprisingly short deliberation by the College of Cardinals, the new leader of the largest religious body in the world spoke these words:

"Dear brothers and sisters, after the great Pope John Paul II, the cardinals have elected me -- a simple, humble worker in the vineyard of the Lord. The fact that the Lord can work and act even with insufficient means consoles me, and above all I entrust myself to your prayers."

Cardinal Joseph Ratizinger, Pope Benedict XVI, knows it is *not about him.*

LEADERSHIP APPLICATION

Golden Principle Number Seven

It's not about me.

1. *What leader do you know who does a good job of applying this principle?*

2. *What two or three specific things do they do to live out this principle?*

3. *What challenges do you face in living out this principle?*

4. *What two or three specific things can you begin doing in order to better live out this principle?*

Golden Principle Number Eight

Sometimes peers make the best leaders.

And Kaibab makes two…

Alex was a great dog. Indeed, our first rescued Golden became the benchmark against which all our other dogs have been measured. We rapidly realized that Alex had been through considerable training. When we walked him, he automatically assumed the classic "heel" position, to the left and slightly behind the one of us who had his leash. We found out from one of our early trips with Alex to our vet that Alex knew hand signals – once we learned from the vet what they were, we could have Alex sit, heel, lay down, even stay for long periods of time by simply showing him the appropriate hand gesture. He was gentle-natured and polite around people, and never did any rude things. He loved being around both children and adults, and was the life of the party.

Alex only had one shortcoming. He hated to be left alone. Whether it was because he had been traumatized by his time alone in the desert before he was rescued, or simply because his breed is typically gregarious, Alex hated to be left by himself. Which was a problem for Lynn and me because we both were working long hours during the day and gone from home. It came to a head the day Lynn arrived home to find Alex in the front yard. He had chewed his way through a mini-blind, forced open a window, scaled our 6-foot block fence and spent the afternoon in the cul-de-sac playing with the neighborhood kids. By the time Lynn got home, Alex was tired and happy to see her, wagging his tail in the yard while she pulled in the driveway. We tried a number of things to corral him. Nothing worked. Our vet finally suggested we get Alex his own dog – a companion to keep him company when we were away.

And that's how our second rescued Golden, Kaibab, came into our lives. Friends of friends were moving, and needed to get rid of a backyard dog they had neglected for several years. When I got to their house, I found Kaibab in the alley behind their yard. She was fat, dirty and mean-spirited.

Although Kaibab also was a Golden Retriever, at first you could hardly tell. In the place of a beautiful golden coat was matted, oily clumpy hair. Instead of the pleasant smile that most Goldens have, she snapped at me the first time I approached her. When I brought her home, Lynn cried. Why would I agree to adopt such an unpleasant dog? Well, Kaibab ended up being our wonderful *Pygmalion* story.

First, she was put on a strict diet. 20 pounds later, a healthy, energetic dog began to appear. Several trips to the groomer where they did the equivalent of a doggie "steam-cleaning" and Kaibab's beautiful coat reappeared (her name, "Kaibab" comes from a rich golden band of sandstone found in the Grand Canyon; once we got her cleaned up, we understood why her previous owners had named her such). With consistent love and a pleasant home, soon Kaibab's snarl turned into the delightful smile of a healthy Golden. Kaibab's life took a turn for the better.

I will never forget one night when Lynn and I were fast asleep in our antique bed. We were awakened by a loud thumping sound. At first it was hard to detect where the sound was coming from, but soon we realized it's origin.

When we first brought Kaibab home, she wouldn't sleep in the house. Having essentially lived in an alley for the prior several years, she was fearful of being trapped inside someplace. Therefore we let her sleep outside, and kept the patio door from our bedroom to the back yard cracked open so she would know she was welcome to come inside and sleep under our high-boy bed, next to Alex.

Over a period of several months, Kaibab moved from sleeping outside, to sleeping outside with her head inside the door, to sleeping inside with her head outside the door, to sleeping inside right next to the door, to sleeping halfway between the door and the bed. The night we heard the thumping we finally discovered its source when we couldn't find Kaibab sleeping near the outside door. The sound was coming from under our bed. Our new dog was fast asleep, right next to Alex, snoring and wagging her tail at the same time. I can't help but believe that she was dreaming of her new life, where she was loved, protected and welcomed. Kaibab had cashed in her chips.

But Kaibab had some bad habits. Perhaps more importantly, Kaibab didn't have any good habits. She didn't know to walk on my left. She didn't know to not strain at the end of the leash. She didn't know not to put her paws up on the counter. She didn't know how to sit, lay down, stay. Kaibab didn't know any of the things a good dog should know. The bad news was that we didn't know how to train her. While on the one hand we had a very well trained dog in Alex, on the other hand, we didn't do any of his training – he came fully trained and well-behaved. And so we were at a loss as to how to duplicate his good behaviors in her.

The good news was that we didn't need to train Kaibab. We didn't need to train her because Alex did. We said "sit," Alex sat, and Kaibab watched. And pretty soon she got it. She learned from him. Not only what "sit" meant, but also "down," "down-stay," "come," "no," "off," and a whole variety of other commands. One dog taught the other. Over time, Kaibab replaced her bad habits with good ones. She learned from her peer, who was also her leader.

Every one of our dogs has learned from the others who have gone before. When Alex died, we got Trooper to keep Kaibab from being lonely. Kaibab taught Trooper how to be a good dog. Jodi came to our home from a breeder and had never lived in a house people. Trooper taught Jodi how to be a good dog. Sammi came to live with us from another family that didn't want to deal with her puppy energy. She had a strong will and was wild. But over time, Trooper and Jodi taught Sammi how to be a good dog.

That leads us to Golden Principle number eight:

Sometimes peers make the best leaders.

We learned this principle many years ago when Alex helped us with Kaibab. We didn't have to teach Kaibab because Alex did.

We've see this principle underway again with Redford and Sammi. Because Redford spent the first year of his life without much human interaction, he never learned how to live in a home with people. How was he supposed to respond when there was noise? When teenagers were coming and going? When the stereo was loud or friends were over? When doors were slammed? When voices got raised? And so he watched Sammi. The fact that she was relaxed and took it all in easily made it easier for him. Maybe most importantly, she was showing this dog who never played how to play. She brought me the ball, and he saw us play. Soon he was playing as well. He saw her wrestling with me on the floor, and he learned it was safe to also wrestle. He saw her respond to our commands, and he learned what it meant to sit, lay down or stay. And most importantly for our heart-wounded dog, Redford slowly learned from Sammi that our home was a safe, fun place because Sammi knew it was so.

To have Sammi training Redford is rather ironic. Sammi was a rescue dog that we didn't want to rescue, and she was definitely a bad dog at first. Dropped off at our house a number of years ago by friends who needed a place for her to stay for " a little while" while they tried to find a new home for this un-trained, self-centered puppy, Sammi never left. After several weeks went by and no word from our friends, Drew, then four years old, announced to us that "Sammi Neillie" was now a part of our family and not leaving.

And so Sammi came to live with us. But not easily at first. She was undoubtedly the worst dog we ever adopted. She had been ignored by her first owners and spoiled by their kids, so she had all sorts of selfish habits. But slowly over time, our other dogs taught her. And slowly over time, she became a good dog. Now she had the responsibility of passing on her good manners to Redford. Peer mentoring of the four-legged variety.

W hat does this mean to you and me?
What this means is that the lack of a position does not mean we don't have a responsibility. The power of informal leadership is the greatest leadership power of all.

There are scores of definitions for leadership. Here are a few:

- *A leader is a visionary.*

- *A leader is one who knows the way, shows the way and goes the way.*

- *A leader is the one who marshals the resources to accomplish the task.*

- *A leader is an encourager.*

- *A leader is one who applies discipline to the process to help team members accomplish their goals.*

All definitions of a leader are valuable and insightful. But there is an even simpler definition:

Leadership is influence.

No less, no more. Leadership is simply the ability for someone to influence the thinking and actions of others in such a way as to help them accomplish the goal.

If leadership is simply influence, all of us are leaders. We lead at work, we lead at home. We lead at church and in a variety of social settings. We lead along the way when we exert our influence.

We don't need a position to make an impact. We all can do more than we think to lead others.

Prior to India's independence, Mahatma Gandhi held no official position of leadership. His leadership in India - leadership that led to the greatest peacetime transfer of power in the history of mankind - was based solely on his informal power; the influence he had over his peers. His power of influence.

For many years Gandhi espoused a peaceful pressure for independence. Not violent protest marches, but peaceful. Not coercion, but persuasion. And at the end, he was successful. India achieved independence. The new nation was established.

As India's spiritual leader, it only made sense that he become the nation's first official leader as well, didn't it? No. At least not according to him. Gandhi understood his great power lay not in a formal position, but in the respect given to him because of who he was.

So here's the history lesson: Gandhi wasn't India's first Prime Minister. In fact, he never served in India's government at all. His close friend Nehru served as India's first Prime Minister. Gandhi simply continued to lead with informal authority - which is the most powerful kind.

Never forget the lesson of Gandhi. You don't need an official position to lead. All you need is the power of your influence.

Sometimes peers make the best leaders.

LEADERSHIP APPLICATION

Golden Principle Number Eight

Sometimes peers make the best leaders.

1. What leader do you know who does a good job of applying this principle?

2. What two or three specific things do they do to live out this principle?

3. What challenges do you face in living out this principle?

4. What two or three specific things can you begin doing in order to better live out this principle?

Golden Principle
Number Nine

Start slow and create momentum.

Raynor the Dog-Sitter…

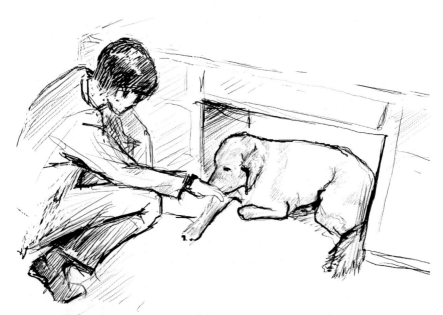

Our family has three kinds of friends. Friends who aren't dog people, friends who think they are dog people but aren't, and friends who truly are dog people.

At our house, the first list is the shortest. Truth of the matter is, if you aren't a dog person, we don't have a whole lot in common, so you may not like being our friends. If you come to our house, you might as well realize there is a good chance you will leave with dog hair on your clothes; despite our best efforts, it floats across the floor in clumps and attaches itself to all our furniture. There is also a good chance that a rubber bone or chewed tennis ball is going to be laid at your feet sometime before you leave. And be careful you don't slip in the kitchen – there is usually a trail of water left on the tile after one of the dogs slobbers their way from the water bowl to their bed. Unless you are a dog person, you probably won't be comfortable in our house.

I don't mind people who aren't dog people. At least you know what you are getting.

The people that I like the least are people who think they are dog people but aren't. Here's what they look like when they come to our house: they walk in the front door, they see we have Golden Retrievers, they immediately stride toward our dogs and start petting their heads roughly, talking to them loudly and patting them hard. Sammi does her best to ignore them. Maggie puts up with them. Redford goes running. Later – much later – he may come out to see them. But not usually.

Real dog people are the only ones that Redford is comfortable with. People like Raynor. Raynor epitomizes what it means to be a dog person. Which is a good thing, since Raynor is a professional dog-sitter. When my family travels, we hire her to come to our home once or twice a day and take care of our pets. While she is at our house, she feeds the dogs and she walks them, but mainly she just hangs out with them. Sounds like a pretty mindless job, doesn't it? Not for Raynor. She is one of the most mindful people I've ever met. The first time she came to our home, she didn't try to convince us she was a dog person by rushing over to the dogs and "bonding" with them. She sat and visited with us. And she waited patiently for the dogs to come to her. Sammi and Maggie came right over. Not Redford. He came more slowly.

When Redford finally did approach Raynor, she turned so that she wasn't facing directly at Redford (dog psychologists will tell you to not "square-up" to a dog who doesn't know you – that movement can be perceived as threatening). She allowed Redford to come up to her side. Her first gesture toward him was not reaching to pet the top of his head. She extended the back of her hand slowly so that he could smell it. Everything she did at that first meeting with Redford was mindful: slow and non-threatening, letting Redford know she was safe. Her next visit she did more of the same. And Redford let her pet him. Their relationship grew slowly. Today, Redford loves Raynor. She tells us he is often the first one at the door when she shows up to dog-sit – he even goes and gets Sammi, who at 13 years old, has become hard of hearing – to let her know that Raynor is at the house. He jumps like a puppy and brings her toys. He plays with her in the backyard. Rarely does she ever find him retreating to his cave. He doesn't need to. He knows he is safe with Raynor.

Raynor is a great example of someone who instinctively understands Golden Principle #9:

Start slow and build momentum.

She was willing to take the time and wait for Redford to come to her. And her patience paid off in big dividends.

T here are some natural leadership applications about effective leaders who don't come in and declare their importance, but come in and take the time to get to know an organization and the team members that report to them.

PricewatershouseCoopers, the international tax and audit advisory firm, and one of the remaining "Big Four" professional service firms, is a world leader in delivering tax and risk management solutions for its clientele. PwC is a partner-led firm - there are currently more than 2000 PwC partners worldwide who own the firm and are responsible for its direction and success.

Unlike several of the firm's competitors that operate under a more traditional hierarchy, PwC's partner model requires building broad consensus in order for key decisions to be implemented. Partners from different parts of the firm, different geographies and different backgrounds all have to agree together for a firm-wide approach to be adopted. As a result, things happen slowly. Painfully slowly. It takes a long time to get any decisions agreed upon. It seems to be a tremendously inefficient model. However, once consensus-building is done, there is real power in this approach.

Because time is taken up front to create ownership across a broad swath of the firm, implementation can happen very quickly. While PwC may start slow, it creates a tremendous amount of momentum. Efficiency is replaced by effectiveness.

PwC's approach reminds me of conversation I had with a manager at another Fortune 500 firm several years ago. He was describing his approach to sales when he said,

> *"I try to teach my salespeople that they have to 'slow down to speed up.'*

> *"What I mean by this is that I make sure they spend a lot of time up front getting to understand their customers and the key issues and drivers that are of concern to these customers. It has to be all about the customer first, not our products and services.*

> *"This initial relationship building can feel slow to a salesperson who wants to go for the close. But I have found when my sales team takes the time initially to really get to know the customer, it ultimately helps the sale to happen faster. Not only is it faster, but they sell more, they sell repeat business, and they have tremendous competitive insulation – customers don't leave, because they don't feel like they've 'been sold to,' they feel like they've been understood.*

> *"The key is slowing down up front to speed up at the back end."*

In other words, *start slow and build momentum.*

Several years ago, a senior manager at Citigroup shared his philosophy on leading new teams:

"Whenever I take a new position or am given respon-sibility for a new team, I try not to come in and over-power them with my ideas and vision. At first I just want to listen.

"As much as possible, I try to go on a 'listening tour' where I meet with as many of the people on my new team as possible, and ask them questions. I want to hear first-hand from them what they think about. What are their concerns, what do they think we do well, what do we need to do better – all of these are giving me valuable information that help me under-stand how I need to lead better.

"Only after I've heard from as many people as possi-ble do I start communicating my vision for the team."

Google is a classic business example of an entire firm that started slow and built momentum. For its first sev-eral years of visibility, Google appeared to simply be an Internet search engine. A good search engine, but just one search engine among a number of competing search engines. But that was only what it appeared to be. While the public face of Google was a simple-yet-powerful search engine, the leaders at Google were slowly building their understanding of the power of search and the best ways to capitalize on the information they could gather from searches and the people who did searches.

Today Google is a $17 billion dollar company that dwarfs all other media companies combined in ad-generated revenues. They started slow, but they've built tremendous momentum.

W hat does this principle look like in the life of a leader?

- Ask first

- Be patient

- Listen carefully

- Be willing to change

- Give up the "little win" today for the "big win" tomorrow

- Make "trust deposits" early in relationships, take "trust withdrawals" later

- Be willing to have limited visibility at first, knowing that the infrastructure for change needs to be firmly in place for any chance to be sustained.

Golden Principle #9 doesn't just have application for business leaders, however. We see this same principle acted out on any athletic field when we see athletes going through their pre-game workouts. They understand the importance of stretching and warming-up their muscles, starting slowly and increasing their activity levels, so that by the time the game begins they are able to run, jump and throw at full speed. The start slow and build momentum.

Any good entertainer or comedian does the same. They start with some small jokes to "warm the audience up," then work their way to the heart of their routine. The bigger jokes work best after the audience has been set up by the smaller jokes.

Jesus taught this principle when he talked about the wise builder who makes sure his foundation is secure.

Any farmer will tell you that you have to do a lot of work in soil prep, weed suppression, ground tilling and seed sowing before you get to enjoy the harvest.

While there are many places this principle needs to be applied, perhaps the most important place is in intimate relationships. Love requires patience. It demands you start slowly. You can't jump to the end. You only get there over time.

Dr. Norm Wakefield is a seminary professor and the author of several family-life books. Additionally, he and his wife Winnie have led marriage retreats for years. Lynn and I were privileged to work alongside the two of them a number of years ago. During their teaching, they shared a poem that captured the power of Golden Principle #9 in marriages. Here is an excerpt from the poem, written by Ruth Senter.

If I really cared...
I wouldn't climb over your walls;
I'd hang around until you let me in the gate.
I wouldn't unlock your secrets;
I'd wait until you handed me the key.

G olden Principle #9: Start slow and build momentum. It works at work. It works at home. It just works.

LEADERSHIP APPLICATION

Golden Principle Number Nine

Start slow and create momentum.

1. What leader do you know who does a good job of applying this principle?

2. What two or three specific things do they do to live out this principle?

3. What challenges do you face in living out this principle?

4. What two or three specific things can you begin doing in order to better live out this principle?

Golden Principle
Number Ten

Change takes time.

Wolf eyes no more.

The final Golden Principle is a very personal one that has taken years to experience: For people to transform their hearts, it takes a tremendous amount of reconditioning. Head adjustment may be relatively easy, but heart transformation is the work of a lifetime.

As I revisit what I've written in this final chapter, Redford has lived with out for almost four years. Lots of time. In that time, his trust has grown. He doesn't automatically make a beeline for one of his "caves" whenever someone comes over. He doesn't run when he hears loud noises. He isn't afraid of me when I come home late at night after a business trip. His heart is getting healthier. I'm reminded of a saying I heard a long time ago: "Love is a four-letter word spelled T-I-M-E." There is no way around it. No shortcuts to get to Redford's heart. No simple fixes or magic potions.

If we want to see the people around us become different, we can't just show up the next day. Or week. Or month. Golden Principle #10, in some respects, is the sum of all nine other principles, and one of those timelessly true axioms whenever you deal with living beings, whether four-legged or two-legged:

Change takes time.

Lots of *Chronos* produces occasional *Kairos*. Another person or animal's ability to change as a result of our love will only happen as we spend time with them. *Chronos* happens to all of us; and in the midst of *Chronos*, when we as parents and spouses and leaders are patient and purposeful, *Kairos* emerges.

CHRONOS  **KAIROS**
Quantity time *Quality time*

Which leads us back to Redford.

Redford came to our home more than three years ago. At first he hid all the time. He wet regularly. He chewed shoes and chairs and purses and wall molding. He would never look us in the eyes. He jumped whenever there was a loud noise. He hated crowds and thunderstorms. He preferred solitude to being with us.

In many respects, he was the antithesis of what a Golden Retriever is supposed to epitomize. To be honest, I'm not completely sure we would have adopted him if we had known what we were getting ourselves in for.

But Redford changed. Slowly. Not in a few days or even in a few weeks. Months went by. Lots of *Chronos*.

Redford started coming out of his shell. He started not hiding so much. He never wets in the house anymore. The only thing he chews are dog bones, tennis balls and the occasional other pet that happens to be in proximity when he is feeling particularly playful (okay, we still lose a shoe or two, but always Lynn or Drew's expensive ones – his taste has become more discriminating). He's still not crazy about loud noises, but that's okay, neither is Lynn, which explains why I rarely get the privilege of cranking up the home stereo they way it was meant to be cranked up.

And his eyes – what a wonderful, wonderful change.

There was an award-winning picture on the cover of National Geographic years ago of a young orphan girl with hauntingly beautiful eyes. Eyes that riveted you to your chair. Eyes that kept you coming back to look again at that magazine cover. Eyes that appeared to burn into your very soul.

Redford's eyes are like that. In fact, unlike most Goldens who have brown eyes, Redford's eyes are deep gold. They look like the eyes of a wise sage; eyes that have seen more then any dog's eyes should have to see. Eyes that could also burn into your very soul. But it was months before we ever knew his eyes were so beautiful. He wouldn't look us in the eyes.

Shortly after Redford came into our home, we asked our dog trainer why we could never make eye contact with him. She explained that dogs have developed a very complex way to communicate. Since they can't use the spoken word, they "talk" in other ways. The play-bow, a wagging tail or tail between the legs, ears back or forward – all of these are the language of a dog. The eyes are one of the most intimate ways a dog communicates. When a dog is scared, intimidated or diminished in any way, the dog drops it's head and looks down. Like Redford did for months. It was if he was a lonely wolf, unable to trust anyone or anything.

A couple of years ago I had the great idea of doing a family photo for Christmas; Drew was entering high school, and I wanted one that would memorialize our family at that important stage in her life. Denny Collins is a good friend and a great professional photographer, so I asked Denny if he would come to our home and take the picture. We discussed setting up several different shots: out front with our house framed in the background, in our living room, a casual one on the back porch and at least one with our pets.

But Denny has one rule: he doesn't shoot pets. You see, Denny is a perfectionist – a great attribute for someone who makes a living taking high-quality pictures for Fortune 500 firms, as Denny does. Not such a great attribute when we wanted our dogs included in a Christmas photo, because dogs rarely do well being patient holding positions for multiple photo shots and various lighting exposures.

Fortunately, Denny is a gracious person, and also a very gentle soul. Gentle enough that Redford and Denny connected during the photo shoot.

Denny was patient and quiet. He respected Redford's space and kept his voice calm when he first came into our home. Denny took the time to allow Redford to approach him. Several hours into our photo shoot, despite the big light boxes, large camera equipment and bright flashes of the strobes, Redford wasn't hiding away. He was right there in the midst of our family, and affectionate toward Denny.

Denny was also gracious enough that he consented to include the dogs in a few of the shots. For one of his shots, Denny suggested that he take his camera and strobe light to our upstairs landing and shoot down into our family room, where he arranged all of us on the floor with pillows and the dogs. It ended up being a confused, convoluted process. Denny's perfectionism came out, and we couldn't ever quite get the pillows, human bodies and dog bodies in the right positions.

Quite a bit of time went by. Finally Denny felt he had it right. He had all of us smile, and he called Redford's name. The strobe flashed, the camera clicked, and Denny called it a shot.

Several weeks later, Denny got the photos back from the developer. All of Denny's work was wonderful. One of his photos graces a wall in our entry hallway today. But the picture that captured my heart the most was what had been the frustrating convoluted shot on the family room floor.

When Denny called Redford's name for that picture, Redford looked up, and in that moment I knew he was being healed. In the place of a dog who wouldn't make eye contact was a beautiful Golden looking squarely into the camera lens, exposing his beautiful golden eyes to Denny's probing inquiry. Redford had wolf eyes no more.

Redford had learned to trust.

About the Author

Andy Neillie is a senior training consultant for Richardson, where he works with Fortune 500 and Global 1000 companies to improve sales and management effectiveness. Andy started out as a high school teacher and coach (at the same time he and his wife rescued Alex, their first Golden Retriever) before transitioning into sales and marketing work in the late 1980s. After receiving his Masters of Divinity from Western Seminary, Andy completed his Doctor of Ministry from Phoenix Seminary, where he was challenged to deeply examine effective personal leadership. Along the way, Andy and his family have rescued 11 free pets (that cost them a lot) and bought one (that's been the least expensive of all).

For information about speaking engagements and seminars, visit:

www.AndyNeillie.com
www.TheGoldenPrinciples.org

Redford